Unusual
PROPHECIES
Being FULFILLED

PROPHETIC SERIES | BOOK EIGHT

UNDERSTANDING *the* PROPHETIC TIMES *and* SEASONS WE ARE IN

Unusual
Prophecies
Being Fulfilled

THE SEAL OF SATAN
The Mysterious Mark *and* Number
of the Coming Antichrist

Perry Stone

UNUSUAL PROPHECIES BEING FULFILLED by Perry Stone, Jr.
Published by Voice of Evangelism Ministries
P. O. Box 3595
Cleveland, TN 37320
www.voe.org

This is the eighth book in a series written by Perry Stone under the title, *Unusual Prophecies Being Fulfilled*. Other Books are:

Book 1: Unusual Prophecies: Tsunamis, Volcanoes, and Earthquakes in Prophecy

Book 2: Unusual Prophecies: Islamic Prophecies and Terrorism Against America

Book 3: Unusual Prophecies: America's Amazing Prophetic Cycles and Patterns

Book 4: Unusual Prophecies: The Pope, the Eagle, and the Iron Sickle

Book 5: Unusual Prophecies: Jerusalem's Mysterious Connection to the Garden of Eden

Book 6: Unusual Prophecies: Prophecies Being Fulfilled Inside Israel

Book 7: Unusual Prophecies: Understanding the Prophetic Times and Seasons We Are In

The International Offices of the Voice of Evangelism
P. O. Box 3595
Cleveland, TN 37320
423.478.3456
www.voe.org

Contents

A Special Dedication

In each book that I write, I take a page at the beginning for a special dedication to a person who has impacted my life in some manner, or inspired me to research the subject upon which I am writing. I wish to dedicate this book to a large group of people who will never see or read this dedication. They have already passed from this world to the next, and all are awaiting the resurrection, when those living will join them in the Heavenly Kingdom (1 Thess. 4:16-17; 1 Cor. 15:52).

This dedication goes to the Christian martyrs who have given their lives for their testimony. These have already gained victory over the future beast and his system, and will receive a special reward for giving their lives for Christ. May those who are still living at the time of the eighth and final prophetic kingdom never receive the mark—that is, the name and the number of the beast—but be willing to "love not their lives even unto death" and, in the process, overcome the seal of Satan by the blood of the Lamb and the word of their testimony!

Sincerely,

Perry Stone, Jr.
Founder, Voice of Evangelism / Host of *Manna-fest*

An Important Introduction

"He causes all, both small and great, rich and poor, free and slave, to receive a mark on their right hand or on their foreheads, and that no one may buy or sell except one who has the mark or the name of the beast, or the number of his name. Here is wisdom. Let him who has understanding calculate the number of the beast, for it is the number of a man: His number is 666."

- Rev. 13:16-18 (NKJV)

Those Scriptures, penned in the 66th book of the Bible and written by the Apostle John around 95 A.D., are two of the most well known, yet least understood, of any Scriptures among the 31,102 verses in the traditional 1611 King James translation. In part, this lack of understanding is due to centuries-old questions, such as how could this particular system of economic control place a mark or a number on the right hand or forehead of every person throughout the entire world?

According to demographers, the estimated population in John's day was around two hundred million. Imagine the time and financial resources needed when John received this revelation in 95 A.D., if all people had to receive an economic mark—which would likely have been a tattoo—in their right hand or forehead. In earlier days, people never dreamed that the day would come when technology would be so advanced that governments, markets, and individuals in a world population of nearly seven billion would be linked by high speed computers, cell phones, and Internet.

We are also the first generation since 95 A.D. to witness the merging of nations into a global form of government (sometimes referred to as the new world order), where nations will eventually give up their sovereignty to form regional coalitions based upon ethnic, tribal, and religious units. The revolutions and uprisings in the Middle East also bring with them the possibility of the reunification of an Islamic Caliphate that will dominate the oil wells and transportation lanes in the Gulf region. Without question, this generation has the technology available to monitor, track, and mark the movement of individuals globally.

A second and often more perplexing question throughout history has been: what is the meaning of the numbers 666? There have been numerous interpretations throughout history, as people have attempted to unlock these mysterious numbers that are identified as the number of the beast, or the number of a man whom early fathers and theologians called the Antichrist (1 John 2:18, 22; Rev. 13:1-2).

Counting the number (the KJV) or calculating the number (NKJV) that is linked to this man may seem odd to the western mind, as we have no western method of calculating the number of a person's name. However, in one chapter in this book, I will explain the Hebrew and Greek system used in early history, which taught that each letter of their alphabet has a numerical value, and these letters can be interchanged to represent numbers. Among Jewish rabbis this system is called gematria. They use this system to calculate the numerical equivalency of the individual Hebrew letters, words, and phrases, thus revealing how they interconnect and often conceal a hidden meaning.

This system of interchanging letters for numbers and numbers for letters would have been known in the Apostle John's day. It was also a method that could be used to conceal certain information. Yet, we are told that through wisdom, we are to "calculate the number of the beast, for it is the number of a man" (Rev. 13:18). We will explore both the calculation methods and various names that, throughout history, were believed to add up to 666. Included is a theory espoused by former Muslims who say that the original numbers were three Greek letters that can also be symbols linked with the Islamic religion.

Then there is the bewildering question: why will there be a requirement that a mark be placed upon the followers of those living at the time of the Antichrist? What will occur in the future that will demand that the world's population be segregated between those who faithfully follow the military, political, economic, and religious policies of the Antichrist, from those who refuse? And why will the dissenters be rounded up and executed through the method of beheading, as indicated in Revelation 20:4?

The answer lies in the fascinating visions that were revealed to and then recorded by Biblical prophets. There will be natural disasters, cosmic upheavals, famine, and economic troubles that will inspire one man to seize the oil lanes in the Middle East and initiate the reunification of an Islamic Caliphate. This will trigger a call to unite men under one religion and one economic system. Since 1992, I have taught extensively about the link between the Islamic Middle East nations and this final and eighth kingdom mentioned in Revelation 17.

According to John's vision of the apocalypse in the book of Revelation, any individual who receives this mark in their right hand or forehead will have spiritually sealed their eternal doom. This mark will essentially be the *seal of Satan*. In the same book of Revelation, John wrote of a special seal of God that protects a large Jewish remnant during the rise of the kingdom of the Antichrist (Rev. 7:2). The mark of the beast is the enemy's counterfeit to this seal of God. It is the mark of destruction—a seal of death that, once received, separates the person from the Kingdom of God for eternity.

This leads to yet another question. Why would the Almighty condemn a person to eternal separation from Him, simply for receiving a mark on their flesh so that they might buy and sell food and other items during a time of great tribulation (Rev. 13:16, 17 and 20:4)? It is a normal human desire to feed yourself when you are hungry, and to make necessary arrangements to provide for your loved ones and cherished friends. Why would God judge a person for receiving a mark to buy or sell when trouble is breaking out across the earth, and the only method of survival is to make use of this man's name, number, or mark?

The answer is that this mark will be issued and controlled by a religious leader (Rev. 13:11-18), and is linked to the worship of a manmade image (the Greek word is "icon") called the "image of the beast" (Rev. 13:14-15). Thus the mark is more than a system of economic control. It is an outward symbol that identifies a person as a follower of both the Antichrist and his religion. It indicates the ultimate form of idolatry and religious deception.

The events in the Middle East and Israel, the global economic crisis and subsequent agreements, and the coming food, water, and oil crisis are like thunder before a major storm. The early warning signs have begun. Let us begin an in-depth journey into the Bible's most famous, yet least understood prophecy: the mark of the beast, and how we are the first generation to see the signs coming to pass!

CHAPTER 1

Apocalyptic Predictions: The Impossible Is Now Possible

"And he said to me, "Do not seal the words of the prophecy of this book, for the time is at hand."

- Rev. 22:10 (NKJV)

Let us travel back in time nearly 2,000 years. Imagine that you are a God-chosen prophetic visionary whose spiritual eyes have been opened to peer into time and space, to observe events that will transpire hundreds or thousands of years in the future. You live in a small, simple house constructed from stones or mud bricks, with a roof of hewed logs held together by a simple mud mixture of straw and twigs. Your floor is the dirt of the earth; or perhaps if you can afford it, a floor layered with beautiful hand-cut mosaic stones.

You travel by foot, wearing leather sandals and carrying a wooden staff in your hand. Your clothing is an unadorned robe with a linen belt and a head covering to protect from the intense sun and summer heat, or to provide warmth during the cooler winter months. Occasionally you ride a horse, donkey, or camel for longer destinations. You observe the horse-drawn iron chariots of Rome, and their weapons of bows and arrows, metal swords, and spears.

As you sit on a hill overlooking hundreds of vineyards, you observe a caring shepherd leading his flock of innocent sheep to a flowing stream. You begin your normal prayer time. Within minutes, the presence of the Almighty overwhelms you, and the scene before you fades like the evening sunset as you find yourself in a strange land. You see a vision concerning things to come. Have you ever wondered how a prophet living in such an uncomplicated, primitive manner could find the words to describe a vision of modern weapons and warfare that will occur in the future? How would the elderly Apostle John describe a modern military helicopter? Would the front of the object look like a massive insect with large eyes? Could the rotors on top, spinning at high speed, appear in the imaginative insight of the prophet as a crown on the head of this large object? If the ancient prophet saw these helicopters mounted with guns on the front and back, firing bullets from the sky towards the earth, how would he describe this? Is it possible to describe modern technology and military weaponry that you have never before seen? The answer is that John would chronicle what he saw by using words or objects he was familiar with in his day.

For example, in Revelation chapter 9, John describes locusts that are released from the bottomless pit (a chamber under the earth) that go forth to torment men for five months (Rev. 9:10). The odd observation is that these locusts do not hurt the grass or trees as ordinary locusts do (Rev. 9:4). In Revelation 9:7-9 they are described as horses prepared for battle with iron breastplates (meaning they are covered with metal). The locusts had crowns that looked something like gold and they had faces of men (9:7). The wings made a loud noise like chariots going to battle (9:9). They had tails like scorpions and the stinger was in the tail (9:10).

Many evangelical scholars believe these locusts are some type of supernatural creatures that are now restrained somewhere under the earth, to be released during the tribulation, as they have an angelic king over them called Apollyon, meaning *destruction* (Rev. 9:11).

Others, who believe the book of Revelation was fulfilled throughout history, teach that this symbolism is a reference to the Muslim Turks or to an Islamic horde that, during the twelfth through the eighteenth century, rode horses, wore turbans, and shot their rifles by turning backwards as they rode forward.

Still others contend that John may have been describing modern military helicopters or some future flying weapon that will emerge out of underground military facilities, as these locusts harm only people and not the grass and trees. To some this last interpretation is considered imaginative and quite a stretch. But the original point is this: how would John describe modern technology, such as helicopters, if he saw them in his apocalyptic vision? Numerous prophetic passages have been written which had no logical way to be fulfilled during the time the prophecy was given, nor could they have been fulfilled for many generations that followed. Three examples are found in the book of Revelation.

Every Eye Shall See

In Revelation 1:7, John predicted that Christ would return to earth and that "every eye shall see Him." In the time of John, the Roman Empire consisted of many nations around the Mediterranean Sea, including parts of Northern Africa, Western Europe, and Asia Minor (Turkey and Greece). At its peak, the Roman Empire was estimated to have a population of anywhere from seventy million to one hundred million people. When

John inscribed these words, how would it have been possible for every eye to see Christ at His coming? If Christ appeared over Israel, He could not have been seen in Spain.

When John saw Christ returning with the armies of heaven in Revelation 19, Christ was headed to Israel to seize possession of Jerusalem and to capture the Antichrist and the false prophet, expel them from Jerusalem, and seal their doom (Zech. 14:4; Rev. 19:11-21). In John's day, it would have been impossible for one man, Christ, to be in one specific location and to be seen *at the same time* by people hundreds or thousands of miles away. But today it is possible.

Two modern inventions now make it possible for every eye to see Christ's return. Today, the eyes of the world are linked together through satellite and the Internet. In America, we can sit in the comfort of our living rooms, sipping our favorite coffee and munching on a sandwich, while glued to a screen and watching a riot, a revolution, or a war unfold in real time. Cable and satellite news channels offer 24-hour, non-stop breaking news from anywhere on the planet. With cell phone cameras and social networking sites, word of any breaking news event spreads within seconds of its occurrence!

It is yet to be seen what new invention or advanced technology lies just over the horizon. When Christ returns to the Mount of Olives in Jerusalem (Zech 14:4), any news cameras can, at that moment, film live images and send them instantly across the globe, where anyone watching on a screen or a computer can witness the return of the Messiah! Christ's return will occur in connection with the battle of Armageddon (Rev. 16:16), and thus the focus of all global journalism will be on Israel and this "mother of all battles." What was impossible in John's day is possible in ours!

Gone in Sixty Minutes

A second prediction that would have been impossible in John's time is that a certain Mystery Babylon, the city ruling over the kings of the earth, will be destroyed in one hour's time (Rev. 18:10, 17-19). Most scholars note that the city John referred to was Rome. This city was the headquarters for the Roman emperor and the Imperial Roman Empire that ruled over the nations in John's day.

Also, one of the Jewish cryptic names for Rome was Babylon, as both Babylon and Rome invaded Jerusalem, destroyed the Temple, seized the treasures, and led the Jews into slavery and captivity. In several places in his writing, "City of God," Augustine compared Rome to Babylon. He said that Rome was a "Babylon in the west" and that "Rome herself is like a second Babylon."[1] In Revelation chapters 17 and 18, John predicted the utter destruction of this city, within one hour, by ten future kings whose hearts are set against the city (Rev. 17:16). In John's day, it would have been impossible for a city to burn and be destroyed in one hour. In Roman times, most of the major government buildings were constructed of large stones with marble columns that could never burn in one hour. In fact, the stone wasn't combustible at all.

About thirty-one years before John wrote the book of Revelation, the wicked emperor Nero, on the night of July 18, 64 A.D., was responsible for initiating a fire in the Circus, which was the merchant section of Rome, located between Palatine and Caelian hills. Fueled by the summer winds, the fire burned shops and merchandise for six days and seven nights, destroying as much as seventy percent of Rome.[2] Nero blamed Christians for the fire, and it is believed that Paul was later beheaded in Rome as a result of the lie that spread throughout the city, indicting Christians for Rome's fiery disaster.

The city, however, was not destroyed in one hour. The potential for an entire city to be destroyed that quickly was not possible until 1,800 years after John's vision, when the United States demonstrated the power of a weapon of mass destruction called the nuclear bomb. In August of 1945, the United States dropped the first nuclear bombs on the cities of Hiroshima and Nagasaki, Japan. Between 70,000 and 80,000 people were killed immediately in Hiroshima, with another 70,000 injured. Hundreds of thousands of Japanese were affected by these two devastating attacks.[3]

It is now clear that any major city in the world could be destroyed within one hour through the power of such a nuclear weapon. In John's future vision, when the city experiences its destruction, men stand afar off and are in fear because of the smoke coming from the destruction (Rev. 18:18). It is logical that the possible exposure to radiation explains why men stand far away in the distance and are fearful of the smoke, which would be a highly radioactive cloud.

Every Person will Receive a Mark

This brings us to a third prediction found in the apocalypse. How could every person receive a mark in their right hand or forehead, giving them authority to buy and sell? It was not uncommon at the time John wrote the apocalypse for both Greeks and Romans to brand or mark military men, and even place a brand upon slaves. It is believed that some Roman soldiers placed a military tattoo on their skin that identified them with a particular legion or group.[4]

While there is little historical documentation on the military tattoos, the Romans did use a tattoo to mark a slave and condemn criminals.

Many slaves were branded in their foreheads so that, if they fled, people would identify them as a slave. Roman slaves that were sold outside of the country were often forced to bear a tattoo which read, "tax paid," once the seller had paid the export duty on the purchased slave.

Branding on the forehead was also common among those condemned by Rome, as were tattoos placed upon gladiators and even mercenaries.[5] One historical account involves a deacon from Damascus named Theodoret, who was banished to Egypt to work in the copper mines in Palestine. This deacon had supported persecuted Christians and himself was marked on his forehead with a tattoo.[6]

In John's day, it would have required much time and effort to place a tattoo on the forehead or hand of every person in the world, which would have been millions of citizens. Eventually, the Romans considered tattooing a barbaric practice, and history indicates that some Romans wanted their tattoos removed. When Constantine became the Roman Emperor and became a Christian about 330 A.D., he banned facial tattooing and required that a slave or a prisoner be tattooed on the leg or on the hand instead. It is uncertain if he was basing his decision on the warning of Revelation 13:17-18, or if he was simply following his own opinions on the matter.[7]

The prediction from John, the visionary of Patmos, that every man both small and great, rich and poor, free and slave would receive the *mark*, the *name* or the *number* of the beast for economic purposes would have been difficult if not impossible in John's time. But it is not difficult or impossible in our time, considering the fact that we are now identified by numbers instead of by our names, and these numbers can be traced globally through computers.

Known by a Number

Consider the manner in which we are identified. Prior to the introduction of Social Security and the invention of the computer, people were identified simply by their names. They used their name to sign letters, deposit and withdraw money, and purchase goods at a local store. The postmen often delivered mail by using the name and not even a street address. But by the twentieth century, which was over eighteen centuries after John's vision, numbers were used to identify us. Consider all the identification numbers that we use each day. We have:

- a house number, street number, or post office box number for receiving mail
- a license plate number that identifies you as the owner of the vehicle you are driving
- a Social Security number that identifies you as the depositor of the federal tax collected for your future benefits
- a telephone number that identifies your cell phone and home phone
- a drivers license number that verifies your identity and allows you to drive
- a series of numbers for each credit card that identifies you as the purchaser
- bank and savings account numbers that identify your accounts
- PIN numbers that identify you for access to your accounts
- a passport number that identifies you when you travel outside of your country
- students are identified by a student number
- prisoners are identified by a number

- personal checks can be traced by their numbers
- even your date of birth is a series of numbers used for identification

Perhaps you have never thought about all the numbers that hold your identity. These numbers are stored in large computers at work, school, banks, credit card companies, and other important places. I cannot think of a time, from John the Apostle until the twentieth century, where a person would buy or sell using not just a name or a mark, but also a number. It is clear that the use of numbers will be part of the future economic system of the Antichrist:

"And I saw something like a sea of glass mingled with fire, and those who have the victory over the beast, over his image and over his mark and over the number of his name, standing on the sea of glass, having harps of God."

- Rev. 15:2 (NKJV)

Even computers are programmed using two digits—the numbers one and zero in the binary code chain. The combination of these two digits forms the language that is used in all computer programs. At a time of such tremendous advancement in technology, the world of computers is becoming more powerful and even more dangerous. China recently produced the fastest supercomputer in the world, replacing the speed of the fastest supercomputer in the United States, which is housed at a national laboratory in Tennessee. The computer, named Tianhe-1A, has 1.4 times more horsepower than the U.S. supercomputer.[8]

The advent of modern technology provides an answer to how certain prophetic verses will unfold. Our technology-oriented generation may be the very generation that the Almighty showed the prophet Daniel. After experiencing numerous visions related to future empires that would dominate the Mediterranean Sea region (Dan. 7:1-8), the Hebrew prophet in Babylon was told:

> *"But you, O Daniel, shut up the words and seal the Book until the time of the end. [Then] many shall run to and fro and search anxiously [through the Book], and knowledge [of God's purposes as revealed by His prophets] shall be increased and become great."*
>
> - Dan. 12:4 (AMP)

The increase in technology, mixed with spiritual enlightenment, has unlocked the doors of understanding in our generation. Now we see how and why certain once-mysterious prophecies will unfold. We are already marked by numbers. The world will eventually encounter a man who will emerge and control masses of people with his own system of economic domination.

CHAPTER 2

The World Must Go Global

In recent years, among prophetic scholars and students, and even within the secular media, there has been an interest in the coming global government, or as some say, "new world order." In the past, when people mentioned the new world order and global government, they were often labeled conspiracy theorists and were scoffed at by most of the secular media. But since the financial crisis in Greece, Portugal, Spain, and other parts of Europe, and since the towering and unmanageable national U.S. debt, world leaders are no longer mincing their words or meeting only behind closed doors to discuss new currencies and global unity.

It is now quite clear that the nations of the world are interested in uniting the economies of the world under one unit. The biggest disagreement is over who will lead a new global coalition.

The prophets Daniel and John both saw the final kingdom that would form at the end of days. There have been numerous empires and dynasties throughout the 6,000 known years of world history, including many that rose in and around China throughout the nation's secular history. However, the Bible identifies the nations and empires that will have direct dealings with Israel, the Jews, and Jerusalem. Using the symbolism and the interpretations found in Daniel chapters 7 and 8, and by reviewing prophetic history, most evangelical scholars and prophetic teachers can clearly identify the nations of Bible prophecy:

Prophetic Empire	Time it Ruled	Impact upon the Jews
1st: Egyptian	1446 BC - 1016 BC (430 yrs)	Egyptian captivity
2nd: Assyrian	884 BC - 612 BC (272 yrs)	Ten tribes scattered
3rd: Babylonian	606 BC - 539 BC (67 yrs)	Destruction of Jerusalem
4th: Media-Persian	539 BC - 331 BC (208 yrs)	Restored Jerusalem
5th: Grecian	331 BC - 168 BC (163 yrs)	Antiochus seized the Temple
6th: Roman	168 BC - 476 AD (644 yrs)	Destruction of Jerusalem

In time, the Imperial Roman Empire split into two divisions. The western branch eventually was overrun by ten Germanic tribes and was later brought under the dominion of the Roman Catholic Church, whose headquarters is Rome, Italy. The eastern division was set up in Constantinople, Turkey and was identified as the Christian Byzantine Empire. The headquarters city would eventually, in the fifteenth century, be seized by Muslim armies. Both the Roman system and the Byzantine branch continued in the west and east for approximately one thousand years.

At the end of days there will be two more major empire powers that will exist. In Revelation, these can be identified as the seventh and the eighth empires:

"And they are also seven kings, five of whom have fallen, one still exists [and is reigning]; the other [the seventh] has not yet appeared, and when he does arrive, he must stay [but] a brief time. And as for the beast that [once] was, but now is no more, he [himself] is an eighth ruler (king, head), but he is of the seven and belongs to them, and he goes to perdition."

- Rev. 17:10, 11 (AMP)

The five early empires—Egyptian, Assyrian, Babylonian, Media-Persian, and Grecian—were the five kings (kingdoms) that had fallen or were no longer influential. John said that one still exists, which would be the sixth. This was the Roman Empire, which ruled in his time. John then reveals there will be a seventh that will continue for a brief time, followed by an eighth—the final empire of the Antichrist.

The patterns and symbolism of the ancient Roman Empire have continued even through the Republic of America. The United States has numerous parallels to the Imperial Roman Empire, as seen in the flowing list:

- Both were a Republic
- Both had two opposing political parties
- Both had a form of democracy
- Both chose the eagle as the national symbol
- Both had a Capitol Hill where laws were written
- Both had a Senate
- Both used the Roman goddess Libertas as an emblem
- Both established a welfare system (Roman 'doles')
- Both developed suburbs outside the cities
- Both had slaves that were eventually freed
- Both allowed idol worship but persecuted real Christianity
- Both dispersed their military to keep the peace

- Both saw their infrastructure begin to fall apart as debt rose and the people were increasingly taxed
- Both raised their national debt beyond their ability to repay
- Both raised taxes on the middle class
- Both became owned by foreign people and nations

America seems to be following the same patterns of ancient Rome. Some in both the Christian and secular world have predicted that America will eventually collapse because of unsustainable debt and increased taxes, and consequently be overrun by foreign nations.

Consider the following: Rome lost sight of true religion and became tolerant of any and every god in the empire, except Jesus Christ, the God of the Christians. The leaders of the Senate were from the wealthy class and used the poor for their personal political advantage. These same leaders loved money and accepted bribes, eventually raising taxes to an unbearable level to pay for the military, the infrastructure, and government debts. Eventually, foreign tribes seized Italy and brought death to Imperial Rome.

The following describes Rome, but could very well be written about America's debt:

"...by the third century the burden of taxation had become so heavy that it had begun to consume the capital resources of the taxpayer. This was due to the increasing costs of the imperial administration without any corresponding increase in production on the part of the population of the empire..."[1]

"...the increases in taxation coincided with a falling off in production and in manpower. The result was bound to be a heavier weight of taxation for the survivors, and their gradual impoverishment, which, in turn, would cause a decrease in the public revenues."[2]

"...the attempt to enforce the economic and social reforms and to extract as large a revenue as possible from the civilian population led to increased departmentalization of the bureaucracy and also to an increase in the number of the civil service employees…this increased the cost of government. This in turn made the burden of the taxpayers still heavier and, under the declining economic conditions, led to further impoverishment…"[3]

"The crushing load of taxation and obligatory government services proved too great for the producing classes to support. They did not have the wherewithal to raise and support families large enough to maintain, much less increase, their numbers from one generation to the next. Their lives were so burdensome that each of the obligatory occupation groups sought to escape from its status…"[4]

In the 5th century, the decline of the Western Roman Empire with its capital in Rome was complete. At that time the aristocrats from the Senate class of citizens were the only wealthy people remaining in the empire. The farmers had either handed over their lands or sold their properties to the government to keep from facing the high taxes. As A.E.R. Boak points out, "These few grew relatively richer as the middle classes were reduced to beggary and almost disappeared, and the poorer sank to even lower levels of wretchedness…" The apocalyptic Scriptures indicate that, when the eighth empire rules on earth, there will be ten major kings and their nations that will submit to the future Antichrist. There are four regions on earth—the north, south, east, and west. In the prophecies of the time of the end, the south, east, and north are mentioned. But the west is missing. There is much speculation as to why the west is not mentioned in the prophetic Scriptures in both Testaments.

One theory suggests that, by the time the Antichrist sets up his kingdom, the true church of overcomers has been translated to heaven (1 Thess. 4:16-17). The assumption is there are so many Christians in the western hemisphere—particularly America, Canada, and South America—that the west is out of the picture. Those nations will politically and economically collapse soon after the gathering together of the saints (Eph. 1:9-10).

A second theory is that the kingdom of the Antichrist will be strong in Europe, the Middle East, and Asia; thus the west will not be actively involved in the systems of the beast that emerge during the tribulation. However, this theory does away with the literal words *all*: "He causes all to receive a mark" (Rev. 13:16), and "all of the world wondered after the beast" (Rev. 13:3).

A third explanation is that the judgments of the early tribulation or the economic crisis on earth has impacted and brought total devastation to the west. Those remaining are dealing with their own problems and are not connected with the trouble in the eastern half of the world. In the time of John, the west would have been toward Spain. The western world as we know it today was unknown in the time of the prophets.

Debt Causes Transitions and Takeovers

Much of the world is experiencing economic troubles, joblessness, and an increasing debt load. The 2010 riots in Greece brought Europe's economic woes to the world's attention. One crisis after another, such as we have seen with oil, Japan's earthquake and tsunami, the revolutions and troubles in the Middle East, and natural disasters in America and around the globe will have an effect on the world's economies. Those of us who live in America are certainly aware of our own country's jobless rate, mortgage crisis, and staggering national debt and deficit.

The United States of America, and much of the rest of the world, is teetering on the brink of an economic crash. In America, our politicians argue over whether to balance the budget or continue spending and borrowing ourselves out of existence. But secular history is filled with pages of insight that expose the dangers of increasing debts that cannot be repaid. When spending outstrips income and debts cannot be paid, the empire or nation either collapses or is overtaken by a stronger nation or empire. Such can be seen with four major empires of Biblical prophecy—Babylon, Media-Persia, Greece, and Rome.

The Babylonians were the first major global empire of Biblical prophecy. It is believed that King Nebuchadnezzar was the first world leader to place an economic system on a gold standard. The neighbors of the Babylonians were the Persians who accepted loans from the Babylonian government at a 33 ½ percent interest rate. As the years passed, the rate of interest came back to bite the Persians, who were unable to repay a massive debt owed to Babylon. The national debt cost jobs and halted commerce, as the Persians had no gold to pay their creditors.

The Persians planned a successful secret invasion of Babylon, in the time of King Belshazzar, and in one night overthrew the Babylonia kingdom. They seized the throne and cancelled their debts owed to the Babylonians. They also instantly inherited a massive amount of wealth that was stored in the temples and treasuries of Babylon.

The Persians began to build and expand their empire with their new wealth. According to the book of Daniel, the Persians controlled 120 provinces (Daniel 6:1). By canceling their government loans, it freed up huge amounts of gold to both build and offer credit to surrounding nations, such as Greece. In 421 B.C., Sparta borrowed five thousand talents from the Persians to build warships. In 405 B.C., Lysander of Sparta used these ships to destroy the whole Athenian fleet. This event brought Sparta to the forefront among the Greeks.

Eventually, the debt mounted in Greece. The five thousand talents Greece borrowed from the Persians escalated to a debt equal to $37,457.51 over a seven-year period. Years later when the mighty military general of Greece, Alexander the Great, inspected the treasury he discovered $120,000, yet he owed an amount equal to $1.5 million. Alexander decided that the solution was to invade Babylon and take possession of the Media–Persia territory. Alexander's highly trained and motivated army crushed the Medes and Persians, seized the headquarters city of Babylon, and immediately took possession of $440 million in gold. The invasion and overthrow of the Persians brought an immediate cancellation of the debt the Greeks owed the Persians.

The Grecian Empire used their new-found wealth to expand their influence, empire, and power. The Greeks began to build cities in each area of the world they conquered, including Northern and Southern Italy. In each major city, a temple was built, which also served as the bank where a person could acquire a loan with interest. The Roman Federation was headquartered in the center of Italy. The Greeks began to trade with the Romans and were willing to use their wealth to make loans to the Romans for goods purchased. But of course, the money was loaned with interest.

As the Romans borrowed at high interest, eventually they realized they would be unable to pay back their loans. They had expanded and built a large army, and it was only a matter of time until history repeated itself. The Romans thought it necessary to take possession of the land controlled by the Greeks; thus the Roman Empire began to form in the areas where the Greek–Hellenistic government and culture had flourished.

The Romans invaded these cities and were able to cancel their debts and seize the wealth in the temples. In those days, the money of the empires was in the form of gold, silver, and brass coins.

The growing burden of debt incurred by the Roman government eventually created stress on the government and the people of the Roman Empire. The Romans placed great emphasis on their military, which was the best trained and most well-equipped in history. The Romans occupied areas, especially any region where they believed a resistance to their authority could occur. Such a resistance began to heat up in the area now known as Israel. In the year 66 A.D., the Roman armies marched into Israel to squelch the Jewish rebels who were weary of the taxation and heavy financial burden being carried by the common people.

The Jewish revolt failed, and in 70 A.D., the Roman tenth legion used battering rams to collapse the walls surrounding Jerusalem. They entered the sacred Temple compound where the Jewish Temple, with its holy chambers covered with gold, was set to flames. The famous arch of Titus in Rome seems to indicate that the golden and silver treasures of the Hebrews were captured in the invasion and carried away by the Roman army. The wealth of Israel was stored in the Temple chambers and the Romans, desperate for gold and silver to continue financing their army, found a cache of wealth locked in the sacred rooms of the House of God.

All of this history shows that a nation in debt will get control of the debt, cut spending, and extend their time; or keep spending until they have no cash flow in the system and cannot pay their debts. If they continue to spend, it will lead to riots, protests, and the burning down of cities; and eventually, the nation will collapse and be overrun by foreign investors and other nations.

Debt Causes Revolutions and Wars

This overview of four major prophetic empires contains a lesson that many leaders never learn. A nation cannot continue to borrow its way out of debt by printing more money or asking foreign nations to keep investing in their debt. It is true that debt produces income, but it is income for the lender, not the borrower. I am aware of a group of Chinese businessmen who loan their billions of personal dollars to nations for their debts. During one meeting in Europe, they loaned $700 billion to nations that were strapped for money. The catch is that the money is eventually returned by the borrower with interest, and these men are making billions of dollars on the interest alone. If a nation cannot pay back the loan, then these men make agreements to own certain commodities in the nations, such as diamonds, gold, silver, coal mines, land, or valuable buildings.

National and global debt is a match that lights the fire of revolution and civil unrest. There is a trickle-down effect to owing more than you can pay back. Inflation, unemployment, and stifled wages bring stress and anxiety among the general population, who fear they will not have enough income to meet their own monthly obligations. Businesses watch their profits shrink, and they stop hiring. Uncertainly about the future builds on the frustration. Soon the fear of tomorrow causes people to protest and march in their cities, demanding a solution to a problem that is too far gone to solve.

In America, the only answer that some leaders give for their runaway spending is to increase taxes. In the year 1900, the average American worked twenty-two days to pay all their taxes. In 2011, according to the Tax Foundation, the average American worked until April 12 to earn enough to pay their federal, state, and local taxes.

We are told that the Social Security program is in trouble and will be insolvent within a couple of decades or less. The very first recipient of a monthly Social Security check was Ida May Fuller, and the check was issued on January 31, 1940 in the amount of $22.54. She worked three years under the new program, paid $24.75 into Social Security, and lived to be one hundred years old. Her three-year investment generated $22,888.92 in Social Security benefits over a period of the thirty-five years that she collected benefits.[5]

When the Social Security retirement program was initiated, there were forty workers paying taxes for every one retiree who received benefits. Now, there are only 3.3 people working and paying into the program for every one retiree who collects benefits. The low birth rate in America, coupled with the fact that people are living longer, makes it clear that the day will come when there will be more people who are retired than there will be people paying into the system. The Social Security program is expected to be depleted by 2036, while the Medicare program is expected to be depleted by 2024.[6]

Another crisis will come through the increasing number of Americans who are dependent upon various forms government assistance and are not paying any type of federal income tax into the system. Out of a total of 151 million single and joint-filing taxpayers, 65.5 million of them are at such a low income level, they pay no tax whatsoever.

Consider the food stamp program. There are now over forty-three million people in American—over fourteen percent of the population—receiving food stamps. That is an increase of fourteen million people from 2008 to 2011. The government stimulus package provided fifty-eight billion dollars for food stamps, but as the need for assistance increases, the debt level will be raised even higher.

The economic situation has also impacted thousands of non-profit feeding programs across America, as they have more people needing food than they have resources to provide.

What do these numbers show us? Eventually there will be more people expecting a check from the government than there will be government funds available. To compound the problem, the more people who are dependent on government subsidies, the more likely they are to vote for politicians who promise them a check. The society is rapidly moving from a working class of people to a dependent class of people.

Those Americans who have a job will work three hundred days per year to pay expenses related to federal, state, and local taxes, health care, housing, transportation, clothing, and food. They don't have the finances to support more people who are dependent on government. At some point, there will be a breaking point in America. It is only a matter of time.

Riots in Europe and the Middle East

Over the past few months and years, the television screen has been filled with images of protestors who are chanting, breaking windows of businesses, burning tires and cars, and resisting armed police in Greece, Egypt, and other Arab nations. In Greece, an estimated 60,000 people—mostly youth and anarchists—gathered to protest spending cuts required to prevent a collapse of the government. There was a threat that Greece would default on its debt, yet the labor unions who organized the strikes demanded that no cuts be made.The protestors during the 2011 uprising in Egypt demanded that President Hosni Mubarek step down from power after thirty years of rule. While some called this a democratic revolution, they must understand that in the Islamic world, there is no interest among the majority of people in changing over 1400 years of culture, tradition, and history. The majority who desire democracy do not desire democracy as the western world defines it. Those who do desire a western system of government are greatly outnumbered by those who do not.

However, the majority of people in these countries know they are dealing with an economic crisis. Prices had increased seventeen percent due to rises in costs of food and commodities. About forty percent of Egyptians live on less than two dollars a day, and there is high unemployment among the youth.[7] The frustrated younger generation cannot see a hopeful future, and with high prices and no jobs, they are unable to provide even the basic food and necessities.

According to a report from the Arab Labor Organization (ALO), the average unemployment rate in Arab nations is about fourteen percent, which means there are seventeen million unemployed in the Arab nations. The report states that among the Arab youth, the rate is near twenty-five percent in each nation, even though many have some form of higher education. The report also astonished the reader by stating that the unemployment rate in some Arab nations is as high as sixty-six percent![8]

The report addressed the unemployment problem as "failure of development, neglect of critical social aspects, poor economic performance, and inefficiency in education." Another important point is that, among Muslims in the Arab world, it is common to have a very large family. A Muslim man is permitted to have up to four wives if he believes he can care for them, thus allowing the man to conceive children through multiple wives.[9]

The average Arab family has 8.1 children per household, while Americans have 2.2 per family, and that includes children who are born in American hospitals to Mexican mothers. In Great Britain, there are 1.8 children per family. Thus, the Arab and Islamic populations in general are increasing at a rapid rate, which adds to the high unemployment rate among the youth in those nations.

These kinds of problems breed revolts, which breed revolutions and new leaders, many whom become dictators. If the Islamic population continues to grow at this rapid pace and the economic problems continue, there is a possibility that they could initiate a move into the countries surrounding their nations. Those nations, most of which are European, will see an influx of Muslims into their countries, whether legally or through military force and takeover.

This summary of worldwide economic difficulties is not intended to instill fear in the heart of the reader. It is to show how, at some point, the entire world will experience such intense birth pains, that the world will be convinced the only answer is the formation of a global government and economic system. The question is: what will be the primary event or combination of events that will initiate the fulfillment of the many prophetic Scriptures?

CHAPTER 3

The Trigger That Will Initiate The Antichrist System

When Egyptians gathered in Cairo and demanded the removal of President Mubarak, those in the U.S. government who monitor situations in the Middle East admitted, "We knew something would eventually transpire in Egypt, but we did not know what the trigger would be."

I have said that it is often the unexpected events that become the most significant. In the roaring 20s, nobody thought that a 1929 stock market crash would introduce the great depression. America was taken by surprise when Japan's Air Force attacked Pearl Harbor. President Kennedy dealt with the Cuban Missile Crisis; Nixon's presidency was brought down by Watergate; and Carter's administration experienced the Iranian hostage crisis. Ronald Reagan saw the fall of communism in the USSR; the Gulf War was fought under the first President George Bush; an incident with an intern nearly brought down the Clinton presidency; and the second President Bush dealt with the September 11 attacks on America.

The unexpected and unplanned event itself is often the trigger that leads to other events. What will happen when problems such as global debt, food shortages, and an oil crisis occur all at one time?

Revelation 13:11-18 tells us that the beast system will control a person's ability to purchase and sell all items. It will control the process by using a mark, name, or number on the right hand or forehead. The system will initiate one religion and no others will be tolerated. Lastly, the system will set up a method of punishing people by beheading those who resist the system.

What will cause ten kings and their nations to join the kingdom of the Antichrist in one hour's time (Rev. 17:12)? What will be the global trigger to initiate such events? Often scholars and teachers expound upon Biblical predictions, explaining what will happen but seldom revealing the triggers that will initiate events that are penned in the ancient scrolls. I have spent tens of thousands of hours studying the Bible, reading thousands of books, and researching Biblical truths and prophecies. My question has not been *what* will occur, as these enigmas are already divulged within the prophecies. The question is *why* will it occur? Why will a final world dictator invade three North African nations (Dan. 11:41-43), then set up his headquarters in Jerusalem (Dan. 11:45)?

Why would it be necessary to initiate a mark, name, or number for all buying and selling? Why would masses of resisters be exterminated by beheading (Rev. 20:4)? During the final eighth empire of Revelation 17:10-12, several triggers will initiate the fulfillment of the prophecies. Those triggers are linked to food rationing, water shortages, and extended famines and droughts.

A Major Food Crisis

Scripture reveals that throughout Biblical history, several droughts produced severe famines. The first on record was when Abraham entered Canaan Land in the time of a grievous famine and journeyed to Egypt until the end of the crisis (Gen. 12:10). Two generations later, a seven-year famine struck the world, and Joseph prepared grain for seven years, providing food for the survival of the Egyptians and his own Hebrew family (Gen. 41).

In the time of Elijah, Israel experienced a forty-two month famine that was eventually broken through the strong intercession of the prophet (1 Kings 18). In the days of Elisha, a seven-year famine was so severe that people were eating dove's dung and donkey's heads (2 Kings 6). On one occasion a starving mother prepared a meal by boiling her own son (2 Kings 6:26-30). Any famine, if extended long enough, will bring death.

The Biblical predictions concerning the time of the end make it clear that famine and food shortages will be a common occurrence. Early in John's apocalyptic vision, he reveals a major food crisis that is introduced through symbolism by one of the famous four horsemen of the apocalypse.

> *"When He opened the third seal, I heard the third living creature say, "Come and see." So I looked, and behold, a black horse, and he who sat on it had a pair of scales in his hand. "And I heard a voice in the midst of the four living creatures saying, 'A quart of wheat for a denarius, and three quarts of barley for a denarius; and do not harm the oil and the wine.'""*
>
> - Rev. 6:5-6 (NKJV)

In the chronology of the book of Revelation, the final seven years of man's government is a time of tribulation (Dan. 9:27; 12:1-2; Matt. 24:21, 29). This food shortage will develop prior to the Antichrist invading and occupying Jerusalem (Rev. 13). There are details in this verse that reveal just how severe the famine will be. The text speaks of a quart, which is nearly equivalent to our quart measurement, and it represented enough grain for a person for one day. A denarius was a Roman coin given for a full day's work.[1]

In ancient Israel, the barley was normally harvested in the spring (centered around Passover), and wheat was harvested in the early summer (linked with the Feast of Weeks, or Pentecost). In prosperous times, a person could purchase twenty-four measures of barley for one denarius. In the Middle East, bread is a basic and important daily food staple for the family. When the famine of Revelation strikes, wheat and barley will be scarce and will cost an entire day's wages, just for enough grain to feed one person. This indicates rationing, as the black horse rider has a pair of measuring scales in his hand (Rev. 6:5).

This same passage indicates that the oil and wine are not harmed. In both testaments, when oil is mentioned it refers to olive oil derived from the olives. The word wine refers to the grape harvest, as wine is still referred to as wine when it is in grape form on the vine (Amos 9:13). Some ministers who do not take this verse literally, make a metaphor or an allegory of the passage and teach that the oil is the anointing and the wine is the joy of the Lord. However, this is an incorrect view, as the verse clearly deals with a literal future famine and not a spiritual allegory concerning the anointing of the Holy Spirit.

Both olive trees and grape vineyards are scattered throughout Israel and the Mediterranean basin, and are known to be able to endure difficult weather and, at times, limited amounts of rain. Another observation can be made concerning the ability of the oil and wine to survive and not be impacted as will wheat and barley.

The Missing Bees

In October 1996, beekeepers began to notice that the bees in their hives disappeared and never returned. Within twelve months, this was being observed in thirty-five different states without any logical explanation. Bees are important to our food supply, because they pollinate a third of all the foods we eat. Some scientists suggested their disappearance was due to interference from cell phone towers, and others believed the disorder might be linked to pesticides. This missing bee mystery, called "Colony Collapse Disorder," appears to impact the adult honeybee's ability to navigate and return to the hive. Years have passed and the bees are still disappearing at unsustainable rates.[2] Olive tree pollination, however, is determined by weather, temperature, wind, and rain. Olive trees, which produce olive oil, are cross-pollinated and self-fertile. Thus the bees are not needed to pollinate the olive tree. In the case of a grape vineyard, bees are not needed for pollination because they, too, are wind pollinated.

If the pollinating bees continue to disappear, within a few years there will be a major lack of food throughout the earth. These bees have been missing, not only in America, but in many other food producing nations. This scenario is only one possible reason why the oil and wine survive the famine.

Other Causes of Food Shortages

Food costs are rising globally, based upon many other factors. Natural disasters—drought, floods, tsunamis, hurricanes, tornadoes, earthquakes, and volcanic ash—can destroy farming areas and disrupt agricultural production.

In 2011, nuclear accidents contaminated agricultural areas in Japan after the earthquake and tsunami. As this book was being written in 2011, parts of the Mississippi Delta flooded, and the U.S. Army Corps of Engineers blasted open a levee to ease flooding in Illinois and Kentucky. By doing so, they submerged more than two hundred square miles of Missouri farmland. Experts say that the fertile topsoil has likely been gouged away, and mountains of debris have been deposited on the farmland. Farming could be hampered in this area for at least twelve months, and perhaps for years to come. Wheat, corn, and soybeans are grown on this land, and the Missouri Farm Bureau said the damage will likely exceed $100 million in 2011 alone.[3]

About a week after that incident, the Army Corp of Engineers opened another levee to prevent flooding of large Louisiana cities and oil refineries. In the process, small towns and farmland were intentionally flooded. People were told to move out of their homes as though they were not coming back. One farmer looked over his 2,800 acres of soybeans and said, "It's kind of discouraging to look out here and think about all that work and money, and know it is all going to be gone in a few days." Twelve thousands acres of corn and soybeans were destroyed when water poured over the levee.

During this same time, fifteen hundred acres of farmland flooded in Arkansas. In Mississippi, 2,100 square miles were flooded. This has serious implications, because farms in the Midwest and the Mississippi Delta are typically the first in the United States to harvest corn and soybeans. Currently, the supply of grain is already dwindling, and corn inventories will be at a fifteen-year low by the end of August.

Consider the oil situation. From 2008 to 2011, oil prices continued to spike, and rising oil prices raise the cost of shipping food to stores and grain to third world countries. When shortages occur, grain producing nations, especially those overseas, hold onto their supplies, only adding to the shortages in some nations.

In their effort to promote alternative fuels, the U.S. government now requires that ethanol be used in gasoline. Ethanol is made from corn, and much of the corn crop is used for ethanol instead of food and animal feed.[4] In 2010, the United States harvested nearly 400 million tons of grain, of which 126 million tons went to ethanol distilleries. This has caused a rise in corn prices, which in turn raises food prices. Meat costs also increase because of the rising cost of purchasing feed for the animals.

There is also a wheat stem pathogen known as a "wheat rust," that has impacted wheat producing nations in Africa, the Middle East, and Asia. The pathogen can be carried by the wind across borders and impact the wheat crops, causing the grain to wither and dry up. Its strongest presence has been felt in Iran, causing fears in neighboring Pakistan, whose population consumes twenty-two million tons of wheat a year. One farmer from Pakistan was quoted as saying, "If wheat stem rust gets here, we will see famine."

An increase in wheat prices causes terrible repercussions around the world, especially for the poorest people. While Americans spend about ten percent of their income in the grocery store, the poorest two billion people on earth spend fifty to seventy percent of their income on food. An increase in wheat prices means they eat one meal a day instead of two.

The United States has historically come to the aid of the rest of the world by supplying them with food, since America is the world's largest producer of grain. However, the United States no longer has the surplus they once did. Wheat production levels have reached a plateau in Germany, France, and Britain—three of the largest wheat producing nations in Western Europe.

Much of the farmland around the world is being mismanaged and overplowed, which is creating new deserts—particularly in China, Mongolia, and Central Africa. Each year, about 1,400 square miles of land in northern China turns to desert. In some countries, such as Mongolia and

Lesotho, their grain harvest has been reduced by half because of heavy soil losses. Other countries, North Korea and Haiti included, will face famine if they lose international food aid.

Another thing to consider is that the world population is increasing so rapidly that, every day, there are over 200,000 more people to feed. Shortages of food, combined with an increased population, results in a volatile situation geopolitically.

While there are many events that could initiate food shortages and rationing, from the view of Biblical prophets, one cause will be a major drought that will dry up rivers and streams used for crop irrigation.

When the Big Rivers go Dry

The global food crisis predicted in the apocalyptic verses can also come to pass by a natural occurrence that has happened many times throughout world history, and that is drought. During the first forty-two months of the future tribulation (Matt. 24:21, 29; Rev. 7:14), a major drought develops that will be caused by a 1,260-day period of no rain (Rev. 11:6). Imagine three and a half years with no rain! This will cause the entire Euphrates River to completely dry up, thus creating a path for a massive eastern army to march across the riverbed and head toward an Israeli valley called the Valley of Armageddon (Rev. 16:12).

The Euphrates River begins in Turkey and stretches for seventeen hundred miles through the ancient land of Mesopotamia, including Syria and Iraq. Eventually, it empties into the Persian Gulf. Iraq is situated about one hundred miles from the second famous river, the Tigris. Both the Tigris (also called the Hiddekel) and the Euphrates are used for irrigating thousands of farms along the shores of these ancient rivers, both of which date back to the Garden of Eden (Gen. 2:14).

While the apocalypse only mentions the Euphrates River as being dry, there are other prophets in Scripture who saw a major crisis concerning the rivers of Egypt. An interesting prediction was made over 2,600 years ago by a Hebrew prophet named Isaiah. He wrote:

"The LORD will utterly destroy the tongue of the Sea of Egypt; With His mighty wind He will shake His fist over the River, And strike it in the seven streams, And make men cross over dryshod."

- Isaiah 11:15 (NKJV)

In a second prediction, this one made by Ezekiel the prophet, we read:

"Indeed, therefore, I am against you and against your rivers, and I will make the land of Egypt utterly waste and desolate, from Migdol to Syene, as far as the border of Ethiopia. "Neither foot of man shall pass through it nor foot of beast pass through it, and it shall be uninhabited forty years. "I will make the land of Egypt desolate in the midst of the countries that are desolate; and among the cities that are laid waste, her cities shall be desolate forty years; and I will scatter the Egyptians among the nations and disperse them throughout the countries."

- Ezekiel 29:10-12 (NKJV)

Both of these ancient prophecies speak about the rivers of Egypt. The main water source for Egypt is the Nile River which, at over 4,000 miles long, is believed to be the largest river in the world. The White Nile River begins in Uganda and joins the Blue Nile River where they intersect in Sudan. At that point, the two rivers become one and flow through Sudan and into Egypt, where the Nile eventually empties into the Mediterranean Sea.

Waters from the Nile are used for irrigation and travel purposes, so throughout history, ancient cities and civilizations have sprung up around this river. It is no surprise that both the Euphrates and Egypt (Northern Africa) hold evidence of some of the earliest civilizations, as men cannot survive without both water and food.

As far back as 1988, it was observed that a reservoir at Lake Nasser where the Aswan Dam produces power had dropped by eighty-two feet. Part of the problem was that Ethiopia was experiencing a major drought. During times of drought, some of the African nations, such as Kenya and Ethiopia, divert water to use for themselves. During the Ethiopian drought, a quarter million acres of rice fields, totaling twenty-five percent of Egypt's production, were completely cut off.

One event that could make Egypt desolate for up to forty years (Ezek. 29:12) would be if the Nile River were to dry up. The Nile is a life source for food and the shipping of goods and oil that come through the Suez Canal, an international shipping route located in Egypt. The prediction in Ezekiel definitely speaks of the Nile, as it mentions the cities Migdol to Syene and the border of Ethiopia (Ezek. 29:10). The Blue Nile begins in the western portion of Ethiopia.

Isaiah saw seven streams, which were called the seven mouths of the Nile, named by ancient historians as the Pelusiac, the Saitic, the Mendesian, the Buolic, the Sebennytic, the Bolbitine, and the Canopic. He prophesied that the rivers would become so dry that men would cross it dryshod (Isa. 11:15). The Hebrew word for dryshod means "without sandals," and according to

Strong's Concordance, it has the associative meaning of being in poverty, misery, or disgrace. This word alludes to the poverty and misery that will accompany this drought.

According to the prophet Daniel, one of the first major wars that will occur in the first half of the tribulation will be an invasion by the Antichrist and his armies as they take over three nations—Egypt, Libya, and Ethiopia. Daniel recorded this as follows:

"He (the Antichrist) shall also enter the Glorious Land, and many countries shall be overthrown; but these shall escape from his hand: Edom, Moab, and the prominent people of Ammon. "He shall stretch out his hand against the countries, and the land of Egypt shall not escape. "He shall have power over the treasures of gold and silver, and over all the precious things of Egypt; also the Libyans and Ethiopians shall follow at his heels."

- Dan. 11:41-43 (NKJV)

The prophet Isaiah foresaw this same event prior to Daniel when he gave a detailed account of the "cruel lord" (the Antichrist) that would enter Egypt. Isaiah painted a detailed picture of the destruction and a civil war caused by the drying up of the Egyptian River:

"And I will set the Egyptians against the Egyptians: and they shall fight every one against his brother, and every one against his neighbor; city against city, and kingdom against kingdom. "And the spirit of Egypt shall fail in the midst thereof; and I will destroy the counsel thereof: and they shall seek to the idols, and to the charmers, and to them that have

familiar spirits, and to the wizards. "And the Egyptians will I give over into the hand of a cruel lord; and a fierce king shall rule over them, saith the Lord, the LORD of hosts. "And the waters shall fail from the sea, and the river shall be wasted and dried up. "And they shall turn the rivers far away; and the brooks of defense shall be emptied and dried up: the reeds and flags shall wither. "The paper reeds by the brooks, by the mouth of the brooks, and every thing sown by the brooks, shall wither, be driven away, and be no more. "The fishers also shall mourn, and all they that cast angle into the brooks shall lament, and they that spread nets upon the waters shall languish. "Moreover they that work in fine flax, and they that weave networks, shall be confounded. "And they shall be broken in the purposes thereof, all that make sluices and ponds for fish."

- Isaiah 19:2-10 (KJV)

Egypt is a proud nation dating back to antiquity. Internal fighting, with Egyptian turning against Egyptian, could be caused by religious conflicts, such as have already occurred (Muslims verses Coptic Christians), by conflict between Islamic factions (Sunni versus Shiites), or by a struggle for food and water for survival. History tells us that, when the Romans cut off all food supplies to the rebels inside the walls of Jerusalem, the famine became so severe that bands of men broke into homes and assaulted their own brothers in hopes of finding even a morsel of food. Anyone who was not physically thin was believed to be hiding food and was targeted for a home invasion.[5]

In the text we read, "The waters shall fail" (verse 5) and "they shall turn the rivers far away" (verse 6). The turning away of the rivers can allude to the waters being held back or turned back. In contemporary terminology we would say, diverting the waters. With a terrible famine, the waters of the Nile will become more valuable than gold, silver, or oil.

The headwaters of the Blue Nile River originate in Ethiopia, one of the three countries the Antichrist will invade according to Daniel 11:41-43. This has puzzled me, because even with their exports of coffee, livestock, gold, and leather, Ethiopia is a very poor country. However, their greatest assets are the Nile River that flows through there, and the fourteen rivers and streams that pour off the highlands. Both Ethiopia and Sudan depend upon the Nile waters for irrigation and farming.

It is possible that, as the early tribulation famine ensues and the waters, streams, and rivers begin to dry up, much of the Nile in Ethiopia will be diverted (Isa. 19:6), causing the predicted drying up of the Nile in the land of Egypt. Through invasion, the Antichrist will seize the entire Nile delta from Ethiopia to Egypt. Eventually, however, the drought will become so severe that all of Egypt will collapse and it will take forty years for a complete recovery (Ezek. 29:12).

When the Euphrates, the Nile, and other waters of the earth dry up, there will be few places in the ancient Fertile Crescent region where both water and food will be available. However, there is one nation in this region that has a very modern drip irrigation system that draws from huge lakes of underground water that recently have been discovered. That nation is Israel. We know from Biblical prophecy that entire nations of armies will one day march toward the Valley of Megiddo in Israel (Zech. 14:2; Rev. 16:16).

Early ministers often stated that these armies were invading Israel to make one final attempt to destroy the Jewish people. However, throughout her young history since 1948, the Israeli Defense Forces have been successful in defending their nation in six major wars. They also have a large arsenal of high technology self-defense weapons that have never been unleashed on their enemies. I submit to you that one reason, if not the primary reason, that the Antichrist will march into Israel and seize Jerusalem is because of the large amounts of underground water and developed farmland throughout Israel.

I believe the Antichrist will come after the food and water supplies available in Israel. This is further evident when considering that the possible headquarters of the Antichrist the first forty-two months of the tribulation will be in Iraq—former Babylonia—and the Euphrates runs north to south in Iraq. When the river runs dry, men will seek food and water.

Israel's Water and Food

Much of the Middle East is desert, so it is influenced by high temperatures. Generally, rain falls only in certain areas and only at certain times of the year. Israel has experienced serious drought conditions in the past, and at times when we have traveled to Israel, they have been praying for rain. In 2001, the area experienced one of its worst water shortages in modern history after three years of below average rainfall.

During this time, Israel and the surrounding countries of Jordan, Lebanon, and Syria were all competing for a dwindling supply of water. At one point, Lebanon began to illegally divert water from the Hatzbani River in northern Israel. The Hatzbani River contributes twenty-five percent of the water in the Jordan River, which feeds the Sea of Galilee. The Sea of Galilee, also known as Lake Kinneret, is Israel's largest reservoir.

The famous Jordan River begins in the north, with the melting snow on top of Mount Hermon. The water descends the slopes and enters the Hula Valley, where several streams eventually merge into a large stream and come together as the Jordan River. The water flows into the Sea of Galilee, then south to the city of Jericho. The Jordan River divides Israel on the west and the country of Jordan on the east, and the waters are shared by both nations for irrigation purposes. Today you will find hundreds of farms growing fruits and vegetables on either side of the Jordan River in what has become a plush green farming region. In the once desolate and barren area south of Jericho, the heart of the Judean Wilderness, there are now miles of large date trees, vineyards, and other foods that are grown annually. Several years ago a large underground water source, a lake about three miles in circumference, was discovered near the area of Qumran, off the shore of the famous Dead Sea. This fresh water is now being pumped out of the ground; and through an irrigation system, it provides water for the trees and food that grow in the area.

Then, beginning at the southern end of the Dead Sea and heading south toward Aqaba, a person can travel for miles and see nothing but rolling hills of desolate wilderness and beige sand, with a few isolated acacia trees and desert shrubs dotting the landscape.

Suddenly, as though out of nowhere, there appears on the left side of the road large greenhouses where peppers, melons, tomatoes, and other foods are being grown, right in the middle of a bleak land of vast emptiness! There are over fifty farms in the region, laid out for miles in the southern desert of Israel (Isa. 35:1-7).

The first time you see this, you wonder where they are getting the water to irrigate these farms. The answer is that years ago, satellite imagery discovered a massive underground lake in the heart of this solitary wilderness. To the Israelis, this discovery of water was more precious than the oil in the Gulf States. You can't drink oil and it won't irrigate crops! After carving an opening in the sand and drilling down fifteen hundred feet, water came gushing up from its hiding place. Today, a large lake called Sapphire is a visible witness of this water source that is used to irrigate farms in the once barren wasteland of southern Israel.

The Hebrew prophets predicted that Israel would blossom and fill the face of the world with fruit (Isa. 27:6). That is happening today, as Israel exports one-third of its agricultural produce and keeps two-thirds for their own markets. The exports, primarily citrus fruits, provide over twenty-five billion dollars of income. There are presently 531,000 acres of land upon which field crops are being grown. This underground water and the high technology system that is designed to conserve the water help grow crops that provide food for seventy-five percent of Israel's population. In contrast, throughout many of the surrounding Arab countries, much of the farming is done through older methods.

In addition to their underground water and high quality irrigation systems, Israel uses desalination to provide water from the Mediterranean Sea. They are currently constructing one of the world's largest desalination plants near Ashdod, and it is expected to be finished by 2013. Even after years of drought, Israeli citizens still have water, thanks to their ability to manage it properly. Israel could be considered the Silicon Valley of water management technology. It is, therefore, no surprise that Palestinian leaders are including control of Israel's water supply in their demands for a Palestinian state.

The Euphrates River will not be the only major river that will be affected by a terrible drought during the forty-two month famine of the tribulation. That is one reason why it appears that the primary trigger leading to the biggest battle of all time, Armageddon, will be linked to food and water shortages. This is further seen in the fourth apocalyptic horse in Revelation 6:

"So I looked, and behold, a pale horse. And the name of him who sat on it was Death, and Hades followed with him. And power was given to them over a fourth of the earth, to kill with sword, with hunger, with death, and by the beasts of the earth."

- Rev. 6:8 (NKJV)

This pale horse and rider follows the horse of food rationing. The word pale in that verse is the Greek word *chloros*, and it means a green color. It is the same word for green that is used in Revelation 8:7 and 9:4. The imagery is a sickly, pale green color.

The text is revealing, because it mentions that people are dying from hunger, which is associated with food shortages. John also heard that hunger and sword (war and violence) caused by these four spiritual powers would, during this time, cause death to one-fourth of the world's population (Rev. 6:8). If we use the earth's current population figure of nearly seven billion people, one fourth would mean that over 1.7 billion people around the globe would be killed, either by war, famine, beasts of the earth, or other forms of tragic death.

Lester Brown, founder of the Earth Policy Institute, makes some distressing observations about the water shortages that are already affecting food supplies around the world. He says that over half of the world's population live in countries where the water tables are falling.

In the Arab Middle East, their population is growing, but wheat production has decreased and water supplies are dwindling. Farmers overpump for irrigation and aquifers are being depleted. Saudi Arabia, for example, has been growing their own grain for over twenty years; however, they will soon need to import grain because their aquifers for irrigation are nearly depleted. The same thing is happening in China and India, countries that, collectively, are home to approximately 2.5 billion people.

Countries that once exported grain are holding onto it for their own people, thus causing problems for countries that depend on imports. Saudi Arabia, China, and South Korea now lease land from other countries in order to grow grain for their own people. Land in Africa is leased to other countries for $1 an acre, yet many of the people in that nation already depend on food from the U.N. World Food Program.

By the end of 2009, approximately 140 million acres of land throughout the world had been leased to other nations for the purpose of growing grain for their own countries. People who had been farming the land for years lost control of it, with no recourse whatsoever. They were unaware their government had leased out the land until people showed up on the property with farming equipment.

This land acquisition generally includes water rights as well. This means that countries downstream could be affected. One comment made by Lester Brown that will ultimately be prophetic is when he said, "Any water extracted from the upper Nile River basin to irrigate crops in Ethiopia or Sudan, for instance, will not reach Egypt, upending the delicate water politics of the Nile by adding new countries with which Egypt must negotiate."[6]

Brown also said, "We are now so close to the edge that a breakdown in the food system could come at any time. Food is the new oil. Civilization can survive the loss of its oil reserves, but it cannot survive the loss of its soil reserves."

How do People React During a Food Shortage?

The Jewish historian Josephus was an eye witness to the terrible events before and during the time of the destruction of the Temple in 70 A.D. He recorded the events in his book, *Antiquities of the Jews*, under War of the Jews.

He wrote about how the Romans surrounded the city and prevented Jews from entering or exiting. The famine within the borders became so bad that mobs would enter homes and search for food. Anyone who looked physically fit was presumed to have food, while the thin and sickly were ignored. Any house that was shut up would be torn down or broken into as people searched for food. Home invaders broke down doors of homes and literally snatched food from the mouths of those who had even small morsels. The elderly were beaten, women had their hair torn, and infants were held upside down and shaken to remove any food that might be in their mouths.[7]

Wealthy Jews swallowed their gold coins to hide them as they attempted to secretly leave the city through a sewage tunnel. Many of them were caught; and when caught, they were killed. Roman soldiers caught up to five hundred Jews each day, and many were crucified in public view on the walls of the city.

The famine within Jerusalem became so severe that dead bodies lay untouched in the streets. The sight was unbearable. When the Roman General Titus saw the dead bodies and the "putrefaction running about them, he gave a groan; and spreading out his hands to heaven, called God to witness that this was not his doing: and such was the sad case of the city itself."[8]

At some point in the future, not only will there be food shortages, but the cost of food will increase such that the majority of people will be unable to enjoy a normal meal. Shortly after the uprising in Libya, I received a text message from an American missionary traveling in Columbia who said that almost overnight the price of food doubled. While that kind of increase is evidence of greed, it is still a fact that increasing oil prices also raise the cost of delivering the food to stores and restaurants.

Famine, food rationing, and high prices for grain are predicted during the early half of the coming tribulation. People will act in bizarre ways, even resorting to killing one another when they have no food and are starving to death. At this point, governments will step in and take control of the food supply, water supply, and perhaps the oil supply and other forms of commerce.

In the days of the tribulation, this trigger will give occasion for the implementation of a new system of controlling all buying and selling. When the government controls the food, water, oil, and everything else that people must purchase, then everybody becomes subject to the government. This will lead to the mark of the beast. The century old question has been, just what is the mark of the beast?

CHAPTER 4

Technology for the Mark of the Beast

When the Apostle John returned from the island of Patmos with the scroll of the book of Revelation, seven copies were made and distributed to the seven churches mentioned in chapters two and three. The message of the apocalypse was spread among those in the early church during a time of great persecution against Christians. As these persecutions arose, there was great interest in understanding John's prediction of the coming beast empire, and his mention of the mark of the beast. The most intriguing part of the prophecy was where John said to "calculate the number of the beast." In those days, a name could be calculated by using the early alphabet. The majority of the Old Testament was written in the Hebrew language, except for small portions of Ezra and Daniel, which were written in Aramaic. The New Testament was penned in the Koine Greek language. Both of these alphabets have a system in which they can exchange each letter of their alphabet for a number. In Hebrew, it is called gematria, and it is one of the methods that rabbis have used for centuries to discover the mystical interpretation of words, or to hide the meaning of a word using numbers.

This system is what John was alluding to when he told the reader to "count the number of the beast for it is the number of a man" (Rev. 13:18). Instead of naming a man and then giving the numerical value of his name,

John penned three Greek letters and then revealed the total count of the name, without ever identifying the person himself. In the period of the early church, several of the early church fathers attempted to use this system to decode the mysterious name of the beast.

For example, using the Greek system of letters and their numerical values, one of the chief candidates to be named the Antichrist was the vile emperor Nero. He was the first Roman emperor to initiate severe persecution against Christians, and he was responsible for the beheading of Paul in Rome. Eventually, public anger over Nero's tax policies and excessive lifestyle caused him to flee Rome and commit suicide.

Greek Letter	Greek Name	Numeric Value
A, α	Alpha	1
B, β	Beta	2
Γ, γ	Gamma	3
Δ, δ	Delta	4
E, ε	Epsilon	5
		6 is Sigma, ς Final Form

Example of Gematria for Greek Alphabet

Could Nero have been the Antichrist? In Revelation 13, the beast (Antichrist) will have a deadly wound and be healed (Rev. 13:3). Some in the early church, convinced that Nero must have been the Antichrist, were certain he had faked his death and would return as the Antichrist. Others believed Nero really was dead, but would eventually return from the grave as the dreaded "son of perdition" (2 Thess. 2:3).

The name Nero Caesar was Neron Kaiser in Greek, but the numerical value did not add up to 666. To help undergird their theory that Nero was the Antichrist, his name was transliterated into the Hebrew alphabet. Once the individual letters were exchanged for numerical values, the numbers became 666. Here is how they calculated it:

Hebrew Letter	Numerical Value
Nun	50
Resh	200
Vav	6
Nun	50
Kaph	100
Samech	60
Resh	200
Total	666

Saint Jerome, while living in Bethlehem, translated the Greek Scriptures into Latin, which was the language used in the liturgy of the Roman Catholic Church. The numerical value of Nero's name, transliterated into Latin, became 616 instead of 666.

The challenge to authenticate the theory that Nero was the Antichrist falls apart when we consider that he committed suicide twenty-seven years before the book of Revelation was written. And since he died and his body has long returned to dust, he would need to be completely resurrected from the dead and given a new body before he could return as the Antichrist.

Others took the word Titian, which was considered a form of the name Titus, the Roman General who destroyed Jerusalem and the Temple in 70 A.D., and used the numbers of his name to identify him as the Antichrist.

Even Nimrod, who was associated with the tower of Babel, was examined. The phrase, "Nimrod son of Cush" becomes the letters NMRD BN KSH and can total 666. Even the name of Napoleon, the Emperor of France who was friendly with the Jews, desired to prepare a home for the Jewish people, and even stated he would build the Temple if he could gain Palestine, was arranged to total the number 666. Throughout history, it seems that anybody who was thought to be the Antichrist could have his name transliterated to total the numbers 666.

Events in the New Testament, from the time of Christ's birth, to the destruction of the Temple, and finally to the penning of the book of Revelation, occurred during the rule of the Imperial Roman Empire. Roman numerals, a series of letters used to identify numbers, were even used to "prove" that the Antichrist was a Roman from the Roman Empire. When some of these Roman letters are given their respective numerical values, they total 666. However, these letters do not add up to any form of a name:

The Roman Numerals

D	=	500
C	=	100
L	=	50
X	=	10
V	=	5
I	=	1
Total:		666

In some of the older prophetic books of the fifteenth to twentieth centuries, there was a belief that the Roman Church and the Pope were linked to the prophecies in Revelation chapter 13. Because the Roman church used Latin in the liturgy, the word "Lateinos" was examined from the Greek spelling. In a book on Revelation that was written by W.B. Goodbey in 1896, he changed

Greek letters to English, then gave a Greek number value to each English letter and arrived at the numbers 666.

Just as the Roman numerals totaling 666 were supposed to be a cryptic indication that pointed to a Roman link to the coming Antichrist, the word Lateinos was connected to 666. Therefore, it was concluded that the Antichrist would be linked to the Latin, or Roman system. Some of the leading Protestant reformers believed that the Antichrist would be a Roman leader, specifically a Pope from the Roman Catholic Church. Objections later arose when it was pointed out that the correct spelling of the word in Latin would be Latinos, and not Latenios. The correct spelling, after dropping the English letter e, changes the numerical value to 661, rather than 666.

These and many other theories and calculations have existed for a long time. For hundreds of years, the simple interpretation was that the beast was believed to be a leader from the Roman Church who would arise at the time of the end.

The world eventually entered the age of high speed computers and mind-boggling technology. As the world became more interlinked and it was clear that one day there would be a global form of government, many scholars, teachers, and prophetic students began to carefully examine every type of new technology that emerged to see if it could be used in a future buying/selling economic system. The first surge of interest came with the introduction of the barcode.

The Barcode Theory

When the barcode was first introduced to the supermarket industry in 1973, it was openly declared by some to be the system of the Antichrist to control buying and selling. In the United States it was called the UPC, or Universal Product Code, and the intent was to use the code to speed up checkout and prevent cashier errors. The code consists of seven units with four different marks. In a popular book written in 1982, it was taught that the number 666 was hidden within the barcode itself.

During that time, I can recall seeing drawings or images of a person with the barcode stamped or tattooed on the forehead. The theory was that, eventually, a barcode would be placed upon the right hand or the forehead, and individuals would be scanned and identified with their own number. The problem with this theory was that the tattoo would stretch and change in shape, making it difficult to read as the skin wrinkled. Also, I don't know too many people, especially women, who would allow a barcode to be tattooed onto their hand or forehead. Eventually, this theory disappeared as a new one emerged.

The ISO 9000 Theory

In the 1990s, a special product mark called ISO 9000 (International Standards for Organization) was established and placed on 14,000 different products that were linked to a special quality management system. The mark was placed on the outside of the product once quality control had been confirmed. This international standard provided a framework to ensure that products met certain customer requirements. It was reported that Europe would not purchase any product unless it included this special mark.

There were some who immediately concluded that the mark of the beast was now developed. The biggest difficulty with this theory is that the symbol was a quality control mark placed on products; not on people.

The World Wide Web

With the invention of the Internet, also known as the World Wide Web, for the first time the entire globe could be linked together in a matter of seconds via computer. Not only did the web make it possible to research information in a moment's time, but small cameras and microphones could be installed on computers, which allowed an individual to be seen and heard anywhere around the world where that technology was available.

In the beginning, a person was required to type the letters "www" in front of the web address before it could be accessed. Once again, people calculated the numerical value of these letters to determine the web's potential link to the Antichrist. The first letter of each word was w, and in the English language the letter w is the twenty-third letter of the alphabet. The English letter w in Hebrew is the letter vav, which is the sixth letter of the Hebrew alphabet. Thus, when transliterated from English to Hebrew, the letters "www" become "vav, vav, vav," or "6, 6, 6." The problem here is that these are individual six's and not six hundred, sixty, and six as identified in the calculation of Revelation 13:18.

We must, however, consider the power of this technology. The protests that swept like wildfire throughout the Islamic Middle Eastern nations were organized by opposition groups that used the Internet, and specifically social networking sites such as Facebook and Twitter. The Internet connects the entire world through computers and T-1 lines. The world was told that, in the future, our children or grandchildren will go to college at home using computers, and many already do. We were told that we would order groceries, purchase products, and pay our bills online; many already do. All of these are not future possibilities; they are already in use today.

The Right Hand Scanners

Our family vacationed in a major theme park and stayed in one of the park's hotels. When we checked in, we were given a card from which all purchases could be made, recorded, and paid for at the conclusion of the vacation. At the time we were given the card, I wondered what would happen if the card were stolen.

My question was answered the following morning when we entered the huge theme park. Before gaining access, our individual cards were placed in a reader and our right hands were placed in a hand scanner. When I asked what this was for, the park employee said, "We are taking a scan of your hand, and the lines are being transferred to numbers. The information is placed in a strip on your card, so that if your card is lost or stolen and someone tries to use it, their hand will not match yours and they cannot purchase anything."

I later researched these types of scanners and discovered they take ninety different measurements of a person's right hand, including the thickness of the palm and the surface of the hand. These measurements are given individual numbers that can be stored in a computer and transferred to a card. This marks an individual, because each person on earth has their own distinct fingerprints that no one else bears.

Eye scanners are also becoming popular, along with face and voice recognition. Just as a person has a unique and individual fingerprint, we all have patterns in our iris and retina that distinguish us from other people. Even our voice patterns are unique and can be identified by using voice recognition technology.

I was startled at the hand scanning technology, especially when my wife told me that the information on our cards was still intact and usable, three

The Antichrist will headquarter in the Middle East region.

If the honeybees continue to disappear, it could cause a food shortage!

This bar code was incorrectly identified as the mark of the beast in the early 1980s.

In Hebrew, the letters www as in World Wide Web would be vav, vav, vav, or 6-6-6 in numerical value.

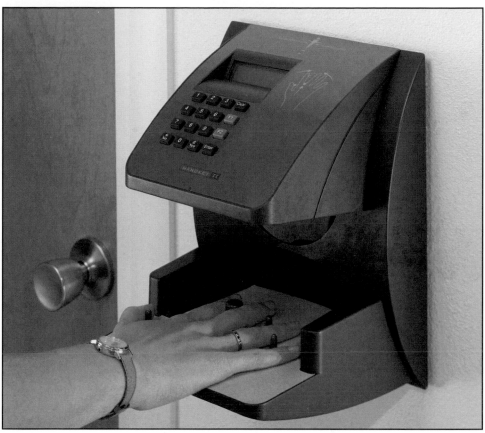

These scanners give the lines on the hand a number that is stored on a card.

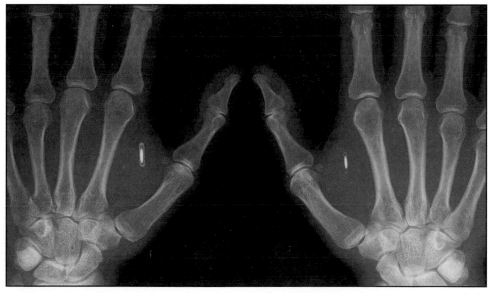

There has been much discussion about placing a chip with tracking information in the hand.

Some suggest the legend of the Golam will be linked to the image of the beast.

China will head up the "kings of the east" during the tribulation.

years after we first received the card. This card told how many times we had been in the park over the past three years, and how many days were still available. These scanners do not use the left hand but the right, perhaps because more people are right-handed.

The human fingerprint marks a person from the time of their birth to death. The scanner technology is already being used in retail stores, both for scanning of products and for credit and debit cards. In a cashless society, the right hand and the numbers linked to these hand scanners could be used for buying, selling, and tracking purchases.

The Chip

About twenty years ago, I showed people an encased glass chip the size of a grain of rice, which held a miniature tracking device that was introduced by a technology company. Its purpose was to track and identify pets and certain farm animals in case they were lost or stolen.

I was ministering in a church when I shared this implantable chip with the congregation and told them that a time would come when it could be implanted in a human. Afterwards, I was invited to pay a visit to a man who was involved in working on satellites and had been working on the Space Shuttle. I spent about three hours with him, listening to his insight. He told me that they had been working on a special chip that was, at that time, on the space shuttle. This man could track the shuttle from his office, and I watched him carry on a brief conversation with one of the men on the shuttle.

He told me that, in the future, this chip would be implanted in the right hand or just below the hairline of every person. This particular chip operated on a lithium battery, and it would be placed in one of those two locations because the body heat from these two areas help keep the battery operative.

Years later, I was told of some of the ways in which the government might convince the public to take these chips. One suggestion would be to use it as a tracking device in the event of abduction. Another would be to mark people who are in the country illegally, which could separate American citizens from possible terrorists. Another suggestion was to store personal health care information. While in Texas, I was informed that about 2.5 million individuals already have this chip implant.

While ministering in Ohio, I learned of a couple in the church whose son worked for a major company in America's Midwest. The company was contacted by Homeland Security and told that every employee would be required to receive a chip implant in their right hand, and only those with the chip would be permitted to work in this facility. The son of this Christian couple felt that any implant in the right hand was too much like the system mentioned in Revelation 13. He told his boss that he would not receive this device. He was threatened with termination from his job until a compromise was made; instead of the chip implant, he was required to carry a card with a gold foil chip on the back. The card cost him several hundred dollars.

Several years ago a large company in Canada was requiring that all employees have implanted in their right hand a small tracking chip that would be used for checking in and out, opening and closing doors, and tracking their whereabouts. Three Pentecostal believers worked for this company and told the leadership that they would not receive the implant, based on religious grounds. After a court case, the three were permitted to be given a special card instead of the embedded chip. The chips are certainly one possibility for use as both a tracking device and a mark that can identify an individual through technology.

The New RFID Tattoos

There is another system that has been developed using RFID (radio frequency identification) ink. This ink, which was invented by a company in Missouri, works in the same fashion as a chip, but uses ink instead. The ink has been tested on both people and animals and is considered safe. A unique aspect is that the ink does not contain any metals and can be invisible. It takes between five and ten seconds, using multiple needles, to tattoo an imprint on the skin of a person or animal. Once the ink has been tattooed on the skin, it can be detected by an electronic reading device up to four feet away. The data is stored in the design and can handle up to a fifteen-digit number.

People currently use these RFID tattoos to do several things, such as open office doors, access computers, and even open doors in their homes. They can also be used in place of credit cards or cash when purchasing items. When the skin is scanned, the information is sent directly to the bank via computer. These tattoos are said to last up to one hundred years.

The Chinese Powder Tag

These tiny chips were invented by Hitachi and measure 0.05 by 0.05 millimeters. They are so tiny that they almost get lost on the fingertips. They are called powder tags, and are sixty times smaller than the previous tags. These tiny chips have a 128–bit ROM for storing a thirty-eight digit number. An article in TechNewsDaily said that an agency has spent $50,000 to set up a system for Head Start to use these tags in tracking children in school. Electron beams are used to place data on the tag, and they are inserted like powder on the hand. They can easily be used to track a crowd of individuals, and are so small that the person would be unaware they were being monitored. These tags can be inserted in paper gift certificates, clothing, food packages, and even money. As tiny as they are, the tags can be read by a scanner ten inches away.

In 2010, WorldNetDaily reported that a California school used $115,000 in stimulus money to purchase chips to track children's movements. The selling point was that they would save teachers three thousand hours in dealing with attendance records. They would be attached to lanyards that the children wear each morning, or they would be placed on their clothes. The report also revealed that, in the state of Missouri, special tracking devices were put on 147 school buses.

For a nation that places such a high value on an individual's right to privacy, Americans are giving it up every day for the sake of safety, convenience, and lower costs.

Identification in India

Both India and China each have over one billion people in their nations. The Indian government announced a program to assign a 16-digit identification number to six hundred million of its people, in order to help expedite food and governmental services to the nation. They have estimated that this system will save four billion dollars a year in corruption costs. They hope to complete the identification number process by the year

2014. The government is also using fingerprints and iris scans, and plans to complete this process of identification between the years 2017 and 2018. The governments of the world desire to mark their citizens, not only for census purposes, but for economic and tracking purposes. Think of all the personal information you carry with you and store at home that could be loaded onto a tiny chip, inserted into your body, and used to identify you: banking information, work history, social security number, date of birth, driver's license information, immigration records, criminal history records, and even a global positioning system to locate you anytime and anywhere.

Many thought this number and the mark were simply for buying and selling, which is the purpose mentioned in Revelation 13:18. However, there is one thing every human being, especially in contemporary nations, uses and needs besides food, and that is health care. What if the government would demand that each of its citizens be implanted with a health care chip or tracking device, and deny health care to those who resist?

CHAPTER 5

The Health Care Tracking Device

When this book went to print, the Health Care Reform Bill had been passed by Congress and signed into law by President Obama. Congress admitted they did not read the bill before they signed it, and in fact, the Speaker of the House was heard on television saying, "We have to pass the bill so we will know what is in it." The bill was passed, and the majority of Americans were not happy when they learned what was in it.

Within the bill were several provisions that raised questions about the intent behind the health care bill. One of those questions was raised about a third of the way into the nearly 2,000 page bill, where it called for the set up and implementation of a National Medical Device registry. Included in the section were words like, "implantable device, surveillance, and unique device identifier." For people who are familiar with the chip and how it will likely be used in the future, this raised more than a few eyebrows.

Was this language in the bill referring to an implantable microchip? After doing more research, it appears that the information in the bill was referring to Food and Drug Administration-approved devices that might by implanted into a person's body. The bill covers any FDA-approved Class III device, and any Class II device that is life-supporting and life-sustaining.

Forty-three percent of medical devices are Class II devices, and they include powered wheelchairs and even some pregnancy test kits. Class III devices are defined as devices that usually sustain or support life and can be implanted. This includes such devices as pacemakers, knee and hip implants, cardiovascular stents, and so forth.

If a medical device is recalled or has a problem that might lead to a recall, there is currently no way to search for a specific lot or locate a device that has been implanted. Most manufacturers have no way to determine which patients have their products. The Medical Device Registry is an automated system that tracks the patient who has received any form of FDA-approved device. The bill requires that the government set up the registry and the standards for tracking.

That being said, we still might not be off the hook with the chip. The implantable medical chip that holds personal information is also considered a medical device. It was approved by the Food and Drug Administration in 2004.

During the health care debate, a personal friend of mine was on a commercial plane, flying from one state to another. He was hoping to rest through the flight, but he found himself seated between a Colonel and a doctor. The doctor struck up a conversation with my friend, a minister, and asked about his line of work. My friend answered and asked in return. The doctor said that he was on his way to a meeting to talk about the health care bill and the new medical implant device. My friend perked up and began inquiring about the device. The doctor informed him that one of the reasons the President wanted to pass the health care bill quickly was to proceed with a medical chip that will be placed in everyone receiving health care.

The doctor explained that work had been done for years on these devices, but that people with certain blood types had difficulty tolerating the chip. They had been working to ensure that all blood types could accept the implant, and the doctor believed that the challenges had now been rectified. The implant, which will contain an individual's medical records, was now ready and would save hundreds of millions of dollars in time and paperwork, as well as reduce the wait in emergency rooms. This would be a major selling point for the public. He also mentioned that the chips would be implanted in hospitals, as people trust their personal physicians.

About this same time, I was ministering in another state and speaking on this implantable device. After the service, a health care professional informed me that their hospital just conducted a special meeting with the people who would be responsible for the medical chip.

Since the passage of the health care bill, the chip implant has gotten quite a bit of attention, even from state legislators. One state Senator told me that he was aware of the chip, and he will do whatever he can to stop it through state legislation. Another lawmaker from Pennsylvania and a House of Delegates member from Virginia expressed concern about these implantable devices. A 2010 article in the *Washington Post* stated:

"The House of Delegates is voting on a bill to protect Virginians from attempts by employers and insurance companies to implant microchips in their bodies against their will. Mark L. Cole, Republican from Fredericksburg, said privacy issues are his chief concern behind his attempts to criminalize the involuntary implantation of microchips. But he said he also shares concerns that the devices could someday be used as the "mark of the beast" described in the book of Revelation..."

The report sadly indicated that some of his colleagues were mocking the Delegate for his concerns and comments, and saying that the voters were not concerned about such things.

Before Joe Biden became Vice President, he was a Senator from Delaware. At a hearing for John Roberts, the man who would become Chief Justice of the Supreme Court, Biden asked Roberts an odd question. The question was, "Can a microscopic tag be implanted in a person's body to track his every movement? There's actual discussion about that. You will rule on that, mark my words, before your tenure is over."[1]

Although the health care reform bill brought the microchip to the forefront, it already has been in use for several years. News clips can be found that date back several years. Dateline NBC aired a report titled, "Life by the Year 2017." The reporter, Tom Costillo, said:

"It's 2017 and you are rushed to the hospital with no identification. But thanks to a microchip under your skin, the information is all there. A data base is growing by the day that collects information on people. In a Chicago grocery store, some people already pay by scanning their fingerprint."[2]

A Florida company holds the patent that covers the complete operation of the radio frequency identification (RFID) microchip and the scanners necessary to read the signals. The first people in the United States to receive the microchip did so on June 10, 2002. Eight people in one family were filmed as they had this "unique identifier" implanted under their skin.

During this time, the Florida company began their consumer launch with a series of thirty-minute commercials on some U.S. cable channels. Here is how it was said to work: For a $200 fee and $10 a month for data storage, you get your own personal chip, the size of the tip of a ballpoint pen, inserted. A handheld scanner can then be used to read the information on the chip. The company wants people to accept it as natural on the basis that it's entirely positive, and everybody should have it done.[3] (Imagine over 300 million people in the United States paying $10 a month, every month, for a chip! Somebody would make billions of dollars a month off data storage alone, should every American be forced to receive it.)

The man who was then-CEO of this company appeared on several news stations to discuss this microchip. One NBC reporter introduced the segment by saying, "Some call it a giant step forward; others are worried about the invasion of privacy it may represent."

On this news report, the CEO of the company was interviewed, and he explained that the chip is the size of a grain of rice. Currently, doctors are injecting it in the upper right arm. He explained, "Information on the chip is a unique identification number. It can be used to hold medical or financial information. You choose what information goes on there, and you choose the type of affiliates, such as emergency rooms, that can have access to that information. The FDA has already given us approval for the chip and the scanner. When people accept it for its applications and its abilities, that is when it will work its way into society. It won't be today, but two, three, five years from now. Slowly but surely, it will work its way into the mainstream."[4] John McKenzie reported on ABC News a few years ago that this company had microchipped 160 deputies in Mexico to help in their fight against crime. These chips controlled access to the country's new criminal investigation center by keeping the wrong people out of areas that contained valuable and sensitive information.

In that same report, the company CEO explained how the microchip works. He said that it gives off a low frequency radio wave, and a scanner reads the chip's identification number and verifies the official's security clearance. "The microchip is tamperproof, it's secure" he said. "No one can take your microchip and use it to their advantage to gain access to your facility."[5]

The chip is glass-encapsulated and designed to remain permanently embedded under the skin. The capsule is covered with a special coating that prevents it from moving around within the body. The company touts the many potential uses in humans. With its 16-digit identification number, it can be programmed to carry all of your medical information, including blood type, allergies, or information on conditions such as Alzheimer's disease. It can be programmed with financial information, and is currently being used for this purpose in places throughout Europe. When information is scanned, the unique identification number is located in a data base which holds all of the information you have chosen to place on the chip.

Since an estimated 4.5 to 5 million Americans have Alzheimer's disease, the company says that real-time global positioning tracking devices are "necessary" for both in-home caregivers and nursing homes alike. In 2005, the company tried, but was rebuffed, when they offered to chip the developmentally disabled residents of a facility in Chattanooga, Tennessee. The company also touts the benefits for people who enjoy outdoor activities and want to be monitored in case of an emergency.[6]

If that isn't enough, the chip can be used in the home for turning on lights and opening doors, hands-free. People say that, even though the chip can be implanted into the muscle between the wrist and the elbow, they prefer the hand because "it's easier to open your door and unlock your car by waving your hand than by wiggling your biceps." The company CEO said they have talked to the government about using the chip for everything from security to replacement for military dog tags.

The newer chips do not operate off a lithium battery. They derive their power from the signal sent by the scanner that reads it. Unlike the chips with a battery, these are designed to transmit indefinitely.

It takes about fifteen minutes to insert the chip. People have been implanted in doctor's offices, at convention booths, and even in European nightclubs.

This is the same chip that is used in animals to identify and return runaway pets. Today, people microchip every animal imaginable—dogs, cats, snakes, alligators, crocodiles, swans, livestock, fish, and horses. Currently, most of these RFID implants are designed to be read only with a scanner that is no more than a few inches or feet away from your body. In order to use it at further distances, it would need to contain a global positional system (GPS). With a global positioning system included in the chip, it can be used to track people miles away, just as cars and cell phones can now be tracked. Currently, tracking devices in cell phones broadcast a signal, even when the owner is not on the phone. People are easily sold on the benefit of this technology, just in case they or their children are ever kidnapped or lost.

First Phase: National Identification Cards

There are millions of Christians in the United States who are grounded in sound Biblical teaching and stay informed about future events as they relate to Biblical prophecy. I believe that if the government attempted to force a chip implant upon its citizens, there would be many who would immediately resist.

The first would be the older, Evangelical community of believers who would see such a law as the early stages of the mark of the beast system. A second group that has already resisted the Health Care Bill is the Amish. They live in their own communities, grow their own food, resist using certain types of modern technology, have their own doctors, and take care of their families and those within their communities.

A third group would be the Orthodox and ultra-Orthodox Jews who are strict observers of the Torah. They would follow the Scriptures given to Moses, which indicate that the Jew should not place any marking upon their skin. Thus, they would be against any type of tattoo on the skin, and would not look favorably upon being forced to place an implanted device in their hand or forehead. Some Jews place upon their heads a small black box called a phylactery that contains Scriptures. They believe their mind belongs to God and not to any government.

Perhaps this explains why, when the Antichrist and false prophet demand the worship of the image of the beast and the placement of the mark on the right hand or forehead, that a huge remnant of Jews will flee Jerusalem to the mountains where they will be supernaturally protected by the Lord during part of the tribulation (see Rev. 12).

When ministering in West Virginia, I met a met a young man from Taiwan. I had mentioned a possible national identification card for America, and this young man reached into his wallet and handed me a plastic card with his photo, name, and general information. I turned the card over and there was a small, square, gold-colored chip. He told me that every person in his home country must carry the card with them at all times. If you are stopped by the police and do not have the card, you are fined and could be sent to jail.

Cards with magnetic chips are already being used in America and around the world. Even newer passports contain a chip that is so small, it is impossible to locate in your passport.

The Chip and the Mark

Scripture tells us that, during the great tribulation, after the Antichrist and the false prophet have demanded that their followers receive the mark, those who comply will develop some kind of physical sores:

> *"So the first went and poured out his bowl upon the earth, and a foul and loathsome sore came upon the men who had the mark of the beast and those who worshiped his image."*
>
> - Revelation 16:2 (NKJV)

Notice this is a sore and not "sores." A person will either receive the mark in their right hand or in the forehead. The word sore seems to indicate that the sore develops on the area where the mark has been tattooed or implanted. In the Greek, the word sore is the word for an outward ulcer. It is the same word used to identify the beggar at the rich man's gate who was full of sores (Luke 16:21). The 1611 King James translation says this is a "noisome and grievous sore." The word noisome is translated to mean harmful and injurious. Thus, it causes injury to the body. It is also a *grievous* sore, which is a Greek word used to describe, in this instance, something that is painful and bad.

What might cause such a sore? At one time, this could have had reference to the lithium batteries that the chips contained, as a lithium battery causes severe burns when it overheats. But the implantable human chips are now powered by the scanners.

Could this verse be a reference to a boil, or even a cancerous sore? In microchipped pets, boils have appeared at the site of the implant. Studies have also linked the microchip implants of pets to highly aggressive tumors. In 2007, it was reported that a series of veterinary and toxicology studies found that the chip had induced fast-growing, lethal tumors in some lab animals, as well as in peoples' pets. Again, the tumors appear in the area where the microchip has been implanted.[7,8] Even though the Food and Drug Administration has approved the microchip, they have outlined some potential problems with the device: adverse tissue reactions, electrical hazards, movement of the transponder within the body, compromised information security, and MRI incompatibility. Magnetic frequency fields can cause potentially severe burns in implanted patients who receive an MRI, and the patient must sign an agreement that they will not hold the microchip company responsible for any damages, regardless of the cause.

If the sore mentioned in Revelation is some type of chemical or skin tissue reaction caused by this chip, then the simplest explanation for why the mark will cause a painful skin ulcer is this: judgment is being poured out by God upon those who have the mark and who worship the beast and his image. We read of a similar incident when God sent a plague of painful boils on the rebellious kingdom of Egypt (Exod. 9:9-10).

The anger of the Almighty has risen throughout history, especially when His own people became involved in idolatry. The worship of the Antichrist and the speaking and living icon, called the image, will be the worst time of abomination in the eyes of the Creator. Therefore, the followers of the false prophet and the beast will be stricken with a painful sore from receiving the mark and worshiping a false god.

It does appear that there is a long-term plan to eventually place some form of an implantable identification device in every American, and one day it will happen worldwide. It is possible to think of many scenarios where a national identification card would be helpful or even necessary. But those who understand Biblical prophecy know that this is the beginning of a more sinister type of control in the future. Once the world accepts the card, they will gradually come to accept the value and benefits of having the same information implanted in their bodies in the form of a small chip. Receiving an implanted microchip is too close to the mark of the beast system, and those who understand the future as prophesied prophetically will resist and reject it.

The day is coming when science will have the capability of blending a person's DNA into the chip. One of the leaders in this technology is an Israeli company.[9] Consider that, once a person's DNA is integrated into this chip, this mark will indeed become the number of man.

CHAPTER 6

God's Judgment on the Seal of Satan

Further in the book of Revelation, we find that an angelic announcement is made to warn the earth's inhabitants to refrain from worshipping the image or receiving the mark:

> *"Then a third angel followed them, saying with a loud voice, "If anyone worships the beast and his image, and receives his mark on his forehead or on his hand, "he himself shall also drink of the wine of the wrath of God, which is poured out full strength into the cup of His indignation. He shall be tormented with fire and brimstone in the presence of the holy angels and in the presence of the Lamb. "And the smoke of their torment ascends forever and ever; and they have no rest day or night, who worship the beast and his image, and whoever receives the mark of his name."*
> - Rev. 14:9-11 (NKJV)

In my thousands of hours of Bible study and research, there is one question that I have never seen addressed and have seldom seen examined by prophetic scholars and teachers. That question is this: why would the Lord punish a person for eternity, just for receiving a mark that is necessary to provide provision for their survival? In the natural, it does not seem fair for the Lord to punish a man who is simply trying to buy or sell during the greatest tribulation and time of distress the world has ever known.

As I spent time pondering this, it occurred to me that there will be a religious figure connected with the Antichrist. This person is identified in the symbolism of a lamb with two horns (Rev. 13:11). He is later called the false prophet (Rev. 16:13; 19:20; 20:10). Throughout the New Testament, when the Bible mentions the symbol of a lamb, it always identifies Christ as the "Lamb of God," with the exception of this one passage. The fact that he is a false prophet who is given the symbolism of a lamb would strongly imply that this man is falsely representing some form of the Christian faith, or as I call it, apostate Christianity.

When this false prophet enters Jerusalem and joins the Antichrist, he will introduce the opportunity to unite the Muslims with people of other religions, including those who claim a Christian background. In the Middle East there are individuals who call themselves Christians simply because they are not Muslims. I toured Egypt in the late 1980s and met several men who worked in the hotel where we stayed. Some had Biblical names. When I asked them about their faith, they claimed to be Christian. However, they had never prayed to receive Christ as their Savior, never been baptized in water, and never attended church. They were simply secular Egyptians who did not identify with the Islamic religion and had Christians in their families. Therefore, culturally, they were thought to be Christian.

Why does acceptance of the Antichrist's mark lead to torment with fire and brimstone for the recipients (Rev. 14:11)? The answer is that the person who receives the mark will also be a *worshipper* of the beast and his image (Rev. 14:9). This man will not allow people to engage in any form of commerce or monetary exchange unless they agree to accept him and worship him. Once people agree to worship the beast and his image, they will be permitted to buy and sell by receiving his mark.

This would be the same type of activity recorded in the time of Ahab and Jezebel. During the days of Elijah, there was a severe famine throughout the land and Jezebel was slaying the true prophets. One righteous man in the government, a man named Obadiah, hid a hundred prophets in two caves and secretly provided bread for them during the crisis (1 Kings 18:4, 13).

At the same time, there were 850 prophets of Baal and prophets of the groves that were being fed at Ahab and Jezebel's table (1 Kings 18:19). These were the same prophets that would prophesy to King Ahab the words he wanted to hear instead of the warnings he needed to hear. These men were willing to compromise the potential of being true prophets of God and turning their hearts toward righteousness, just to enjoy food at Jezebel's table in the time of famine. They prophesied whatever was necessary to ensure they would not be slain by Jezebel.

People will engage in bizarre, illegal, and unethical behavior to keep from starving to death. In the days of Elisha, the famine in Samaria was so severe that people were eating dove's dung and donkey's heads (2 Kings 6:25).

The Icon of the Beast

In the Matthew narrative called the Olivet Discourse, Jesus warned of false prophets that would deceive many (Matt. 24:11). Certain counterfeits would even perform false miracles and thereby deceive many. He warned of the danger that even the very elect could be deceived (Matt. 24:24).

Throughout history there have been countless false religious leaders that have drawn away a following for their own personal gain. However, these end time counterfeit spiritual gurus and leaders are so believable and dangerous that they could actually deceive God's elect! In the Bible (the Old Testament), devout Jews are considered God's elect. During the tribulation there are 144,000 Jews sealed with the seal of God, while another Jewish remnant will flee to the wilderness. Two-thirds of those remaining in Israel will die in the tribulation.

What type of miracle could be performed that will cause such deception that even a religiously-minded person could be blinded by the spirit of deception? Since the Bible is a book about spirituality and the miracle could deceive the elect, the false prophet must perform a religiously-oriented miracle to pull in the masses. This miracle is recorded in the vision of John in Revelation 13:

"Then I saw another beast coming up out of the earth, and he had two horns like a lamb and spoke like a dragon. "And he exercises all the authority of the first beast in his presence, and causes the earth and those who dwell in it to worship the first beast, whose deadly wound was healed. "He performs great signs, so that he even makes fire come down from heaven on the earth in the sight of men. "And he deceives those who dwell on the earth by those signs which he was granted to do in the sight of the beast, telling those who dwell on the earth to make an image to the beast who was wounded by the sword and lived. "He was granted power to give breath to the image of the beast, that the image of the beast should both speak and cause as many as would not worship the image of the beast to be killed."

- Revelation 13:11-15 (NKJV)

The first miracle mentioned is "making fire come down from heaven in the sight of men." This is the same type of miracle that was preformed by Elijah on Mount Carmel, when the fire of God fell and consumed the sacrifices, proving that Baal was a powerless false god (1 Kings 18:36-38). This miracle would imply that this man is given some limited authority to control the powers of heaven.

The second miracle, however, is the most dangerous. This involves making and worshipping an image, which is forbidden as idolatry in the Ten Commandments (Exod. 20:3-4). This was also a sin that, on considerable occasions, caused the judgment of God to be unleashed upon Israel.

The coming false prophet will make an image of the beast. The beast in this instance is the Antichrist—the beast mentioned in Revelation 13:1-2. The deadly wound of the Antichrist will be healed and the world will be astonished. The Greek word for image in this passage is *eikon* or, as we would say, *icon*. From a religious perspective, an icon can be a painting or a statue of a religious person, such as Christ, the disciples, early saints, or angels that are venerated or honored in times of worship or prayer. The use of such icons is not found in Protestant churches, and their use was rejected by the Protestant reformers. Icons have been and are still used in the Roman Catholic and Eastern Orthodox churches, which are the prominent churches in Europe and the Middle East.

The icon of the beast is not just a stationary image carved of wood, metal or plastic. Through a powerful demonic manifestation, this image will actually speak and live. Here is something to consider. God himself formed a man, Adam, from dust and caused him to come alive (Gen. 2:7). But even Christ, with a resume of miracles that includes raising Lazarus from the dead (John 11:42-44), never formed an icon and caused it to speak and live.

Much of the world is so ignorant of the true story of Christ's death and resurrection that the miracles of the false prophet could cause him to be given the title of Christ himself. But as believers, we know that the real Christ will have nail prints in His feet and hands (John 20:25-27)!

One reason why God forbids the use of images is because they can be used as a conduit for counterfeit miracles that deceive people. In one of the famous churches in the Holy Land, there was an old painting of Christ's face on one of the columns in the church. Word suddenly spread that the painting was weeping. Immediately, hundreds of locals, followed by thousands of pilgrims, gathered to see this "miracle" and bring their offerings to the church.

A Palestinian friend of mine lived in the community and was friends with the priest and members at the church. I asked him about this alleged miracle. He laughed and said, "The church needed a new roof and the priest had a squirt gun and shot water on the face. He then began telling people, "The face is crying." It drew thousands who left generous donations for the church.

In the first century, the Christian church had no images of Christ or saints. From 100 to 400 A.D., early Christian leaders rebuked those who sought to introduce images in worship. The 36th synod of Elvira prohibited images as a hindrance of worship to God. The early father Eusebius opposed images.

In the time of Augustine, Jerome, and Ambrose, images were introduced in the church—especially the eastern branch of the church. From about the year 766 onward, many leaders in the church not only accepted images, but used them in veneration in worship. This action was and still is a violation of the warnings given by the Almighty in the Scriptures (Exod. 20:4; 34:13; Num. 33:51-53). One of the Ten Commandments is, "You shall not make unto you a graven image" (Exodus 20:4).

The inspired Scriptures also forbid praying to and worshipping idols (1 Kings 18:25-29; 1 Thess. 1:9; 1 John 5:21; Rev. 9:20), burning incense to idols (Isa. 65:3), and kissing or bowing down to an image (1 Kings 19:18; 2 Kings 5:18). Any religious image, regardless of the religion it represents, that appears to bleed, cry, or move is a counterfeit miracle. The Holy Spirit will never go against the revelation and warnings of the Holy Scriptures, and manifest upon an image that God Almighty forbids. These false miracles cause a person to worship the image and be drawn into further acceptance of other images that manifest some form of alleged life.

Is it possible that the emphasis on images in the Roman Church has unknowingly and unwittingly prepared masses of people in Europe and the Middle East to accept a future false miracle of the talking and living image of the beast, especially when the image is built by a religious leader who claims to represent Christianity?

John tells us that this image of the beast will speak and live, causing multitudes to worship the image (icon). When Moses built the brazen serpent in the wilderness, Israel looked on the serpent (which was a picture of Christ on the cross) and people were healed (Num. 21). Israel preserved this brass serpent in the Temple for nine hundred years and burned incense to it. In the time of King Hezekiah, the godly leader destroyed the holy relic because it had become an idol to the Jews (2 Kings 18:4). God hates idolatry.

Those who receive the mark, name, or number of the beast will also *worship* the image of the beast. It appears that this image will be set in Jerusalem at the Temple Mount, since this is the "abomination that makes Jerusalem desolate" (Dan. 9:27; Matt. 24:15). Devout Jews would never worship images or place tattoos on their body, because that is forbidden in the Torah (Exod. 20:4; Lev. 19:28). Thus, when this image begins to speak and live, Jews will flee the city, knowing the miracle is satanic and not from God.

It is the worship of this image and belief in a counterfeit Christ that seals the doom of those who join themselves with this future beast system, because these people will align themselves with the religion of the Antichrist. Even when the wicked ruler Antiochus Epiphanies invaded Israel; placed a swine on the altar; forbade the Jews to worship or celebrate the Sabbath and feasts days; and forbade them to circumcise their children, there were Jews who turned against the covenant and joined with Antiochus to protect themselves and their families.

Right now, most of us sit in the comfort of a home or apartment, with the freedom to drive a vehicle to a local restaurant and enjoy a pleasant meal. Under those circumstances, it is easy to say that you would never compromise your spiritual convictions by bowing to an image or accepting a mark. But when the day that John saw arrives, what will people do in exchange for a guarantee that they will not be killed and food will be provided while others are starving?

The Seal of God

In both Testaments, there are references to God sealing people by placing a mark on their foreheads. The first mention of a mark on the head is in Genesis 4:15. In jealousy, Cain, the oldest son of Adam, slew his brother Abel. The Bible says that God set a mark upon his head so that anyone finding him would not kill him. The Hebrew word used in this verse is *owth* and it means, "a monument, an omen, or a sign."

The Bible does not tell us what kind of mark this was. However, years ago I asked one of Jerusalem's leading rabbis, Yehuda Getz, what the mark was upon Cain's head. He replied, "According to tradition, God marked Cain with the Hebrew letter tav." This is the twenty-second and final letter of the Hebrew alphabet. In the ancient Hebrew alphabet, it was in the form of a + or an x, making the symbol of tav a cross.

In the time of the Babylonian invasion, the Lord instructed one man (an angel) with an inkhorn to go through Jerusalem and place a mark on the foreheads of the righteous men who were crying out to God for the sins and abomination being done in the city. In Ezekiel 9:4 and 9:6, the Hebrew word for the mark placed upon the foreheads is *tav,* the word identifying the last letter of the Hebrew alphabet—but also indicating that the form of the mark would have been a + or an x sign. Again, they were marked with the universal symbol of a cross.

As the inhabitants of Jerusalem were being slain, the righteous men who had the mark upon their foreheads were to be spared (Ezek. 9:6). This is an example of how the mark of God sealed the righteous and protected them from destruction.

The same imagery is used in Revelation chapter 7 concerning 144,000 Jews, or 12,000 men from each of the twelve tribes of Israel. John saw an angel coming from the east, "having the seal of the living God" (Rev. 7:2). The judgment angels cannot harm the earth, grass, or trees until the angels have sealed the servants of God in their foreheads (Rev. 7:3).

In chapter 7, there is no clue to indicate what this seal might be. However, later in Revelation, we see these 144,000 men appearing in the Heavenly Temple worshipping God and the Christ. We read that they have "the Father's name written in their foreheads." While religious Jews would never place a mark on their skin, in this case, it was an angel of the Lord who marked them with a seal of God.

Believers speak of being cleansed or washed by the blood of Christ. However, we never see actual blood washing over our souls to remove sins when we repent. The cleansing process is a spiritual and invisible act that occurs when we believe with our hearts and confess with our mouths that Christ has risen from the dead and His blood brings us redemption. It is our confession that releases the action of the Holy Spirit's forgiveness, cleansing, redemption, and justification (Rom. 10:9-10). The same is true with prayer. We can hear the words we speak, and so can God, even though His heavenly dwelling place is billions of light years from us. We hear words, but don't see the words. Yet there are golden vials in heaven, full of odors which are the prayers of the saints (Rev. 5:8). When these vials are opened, then our prayers come up before God as a memorial and are answered (see Acts 10:1-4).

The protective seal of God in the foreheads of these Jewish men is the Father's name. In the Old Testament, there are many compound names for God. Each name has a particular meaning and reveals a certain characteristic of God's abilities:

Compound Names	Meaning of the Names	Scripture Reference
Jehovah Elohim	The Eternal Creator	Genesis 2:4-25
Adonai Jehovah	The Lord our Master	Genesis 15:2
Jehovah Jirah	The Lord our Provider	Genesis 22:8-14
Jehovah Nissi	The Lord our Banner	Exodus 17:15
Jehovah Ropheka	The Lord our Healer	Exodus 15:26
Jehovah Shalom	The Lord our Peace	Judges 6:24
Jehovah Tsidkienu	The Lord our Righteousness	Jeremiah 23:6
Jehovah Mekaddishkem	The Lord our Sanctifier	Exodus 31:13
Jehovah Sabaoth	The Lord of Hosts	1 Samuel 1:11
Jehovah Shammah	The Lord is Present	Ezekiel 48:35
Jehovah Elyon	The Lord Most High	Psalms 7:17
Jehovah Rohi	The Lord my Shepherd	Psalms 23:1
Jehovah Hoseenu	The Lord our Maker	Psalms 95:6
Jehovah Eloheenu	The Lord our God	Psalms 99:5
Jehovah Eloheka	The Lord thy God	Exodus 20:2
Jehovah Elohay	The Lord my God	Zechariah 14:5

In the Hebrew language, there is one name of the Father that is considered among pious Jews to be so sacred that neither Jewish men nor rabbis will attempt to pronounce it. In English, the name is Jehovah. However, the actual name is spelled with four Hebrew letters: yud, hei, vav and hei (YHWH in English). It is taught in Judaism that no one is certain how to pronounce this name that was first revealed to Moses:

> *"And I appeared unto Abraham, unto Isaac, and unto Jacob, by the name of God Almighty, but by my name JEHOVAH was I not known to them."*
>
> - Exodus 6:3 (KJV)

From the time of Adam to Moses (at 80 years of age), God concealed this name from mankind. This name would become His covenant name forever. Since devout Jews refuse to read this name in the scrolls (they replace it with Adonai), this is perhaps the name that becomes the seal of God in the foreheads. There is no indication that the mark on their heads is visible, as much of our spiritual blessing is initiated by faith and not by sight. It could be possible that the name is revealed to them and concealed in their minds, which the soulish realm of a person. Regardless of what this seal might be, we know it is a seal of God that protects the righteous!

Among Jewish mystics the seal of God is simply truth. In Hebrew the word truth is *emet*, spelled with three Hebrew letters, alef, mem and tav. These are the beginning, middle, and ending letters of the alphabet. God and His Word are absolute truth, and when you abide in truth you have the full protection of God's covenant. The word *emet* has numerous mystical meanings and is also linked to an odd Jewish legend about a creature called a golem.

The Golem Story

One of the theories about the image of the beast is linked to a Jewish story called the legend of the golem. I first heard this legend when I toured Israel in the early 1990s. The Hebrew word golem means "a shapeless mass." The word is used one time in the Old Testament, although Jewish tradition says that Adam was a golem when he was initially formed from the dust. In the following verse, the English phrase for golem is "substance being yet unformed."

"Your eyes saw my substance, being yet unformed, and in your book they all were written, the days fashioned for me, when as yet there were none of them."

– Psalm 139:16 (NKJV)

In the 6th century, a Jewish man wrote a book that contained mystical speculation about creation. The book was called *Sefer Yezirah,* or the *Book of Creation.* The writer speculated that life was created by reciting combinations of letters of the Hebrew alphabet. Hundreds of years after that book was written, some Jewish mystics began to teach that, since God used these letters when He spoke the words that created the universe, humans can wield the same power if they masterfully combine these letters. They also taught that only the most pious and righteous man is able to create life.

The most well-known Jewish legend that involved the creation of life through the fashioning of a golem from clay involved an incident that occurred in the year 1580. Jews who lived in Prague, Czechoslovakia were being greatly persecuted by Christians under the rule of the Roman Emperor

Rudolf II. Jewish enemies had accused the Jews of mixing the blood of non-Jewish children in their flour and water when making unleavened bread. This lie, known as blood libel, incited mobs to retaliate against Jews living in the region.

To protect the Jews, the chief rabbi allegedly formed a figure from clay and shaped it like a human. One legend states that such a figure could be brought to life by writing the Hebrew letters alef, mem, and tav (meaning emet, or truth) on the forehead of the golem. To kill the golem, the rabbi had to remove the letter alef. This left the letters mem and tav, which meant death. Another way to make the golem come to life was to write the name of God on parchment and place the paper in the golem's mouth. To remove life from the golem, one must remove the parchment from its mouth.

When the golem in Prague came to life, the rabbi ordered it to protect the Jews. According to legend, it did just that. But as it became fiercer and more violent, the rabbi took life away from the golem. The clay was placed in the attic of a synagogue in Prague, where according to some, it remains to this day. Some rabbis have advised that nobody ever enter the attic where this clay is kept. Even today, tourists who visit Prague can purchase statues, images, and paintings of golems.[1]

This legend has led some prophetic students to speculate that the future false prophet could be from a Jewish background because a Jewish mystic would be familiar with the legend and would know how to make a golem come to life. Since it required that the letters alef, mem, and tav be placed on the forehead, some believe that could be linked to the mark of the beast. If a series of letters could be placed upon the forehead of the image of the beast, and the false prophet can appear to cause the image to live through some magical combination of letters or words, then perhaps the followers of the beast system would be willing to place the same words on their own foreheads.

While the story of the golem is a legend, there are Jewish rabbis who believe it literally occurred. Some even believe that the golem in Prague—although he most surely would have turned to dust by now—could awaken again when there is a need for justice united with a holy purpose. With advances in the fields of science and technology, along with gene manipulation, it is possible that the day will come when events behind the legend could become more than just folklore.

Cloning

Perhaps you remember Dolly, the lamb that was born in 1997 as a result of genetic cloning by Scottish scientists at the Roslin Institute. Cloning is the creation of an organism that is an exact genetic copy of another. Some form of cloning has existed for over one hundred years—the first example being the cloning of a sea urchin. But Dolly was the first mammal ever to be cloned using a donor nucleus from an adult somatic cell. This lamb brought the controversy of cloning to the forefront.

The birth of Dolly resulted in discussion about the cloning of humans. Perhaps you recall that the cloning debate was also part of the stem cell research debate, as some researchers thought that cloning would be one approach to producing medical stem cells. As a result of this debate, in 1997 the United States temporarily banned the use of taxpayer money to research and fund human cloning. Private agencies were asked to delay cloning research, as it was deemed unethical, irresponsible, and unprofessional. But several private companies continued with their cloning research in spite of the requests.

Most people throughout the world recognize the dangers of cloning and are opposed to it. One group that supports cloning is a religious sect in the United States called the Raelians, who believe that humans are clones created by alien scientists who brought DNA from another planet. They also believe they can seek immortality through cloning.

While a variety of animals have been cloned since the procedure first began, the cloning failure rate is currently very high. Most cloned animals do not survive very long. They are also much larger at birth than animals conceived through the natural method. Cloned animals have much larger organs and various medical conditions that can cause problems later in the animal's life. They also age faster than a normal animal.

The majority of scientists believe that the cloning of human beings is unethical and potentially dangerous. However, that has not stopped some from wanting to try it. An outcry was heard around the world when an Italian doctor named Severino Antinori wanted to produce a human clone by impregnating up to two hundred women with cloned embryos!

Could the image mentioned in Revelation 13:14-15 be a clone? I only mention this as a possibility. With the strange and unusual things science is capable of doing today, many things are a possibility.

Holography

Another unusual technique is currently being used and improved upon that could explain the image of the beast. Most of us are familiar with holograms, because we have seen small holographic images, perhaps on trading cards or credit cards. Holography is a technique that allows light scattered from an object to be recorded and later reconstructed so that when an image system, such as a camera or an eye, is placed in the reconstructed beam, an image of the object will be seen, even when the object is no longer present.

The hologram recreates the light that came from the original scene, and the scene or object can be viewed from different distances and angles. This makes the object appear three-dimensional, and it seems to be right in front of you, even though the object is not actually present. Only the three-dimensional holographic image is present. Some appear to move as you walk past them and view them from different angles. If you cut a hologram in half, each half will still contain the whole view of the entire original image. Holographic images can now appear to float in mid-air, and they are so real that it looks like you can touch them. You can even make them move with your own hand movements.

In 2011, it was reported that the Japanese have found a technique to create full-color holograms, and it was such an important discovery that it could transform 3D television and movies, making it possible to view 3D film without special glasses.

On the night of the 2008 elections, CNN filmed a journalist in Chicago, using thirty-five high definition cameras all around her. The holographic, three-dimensional figure of the journalist was beamed into the studio in New York, where Wolfe Blitzer talked to her as though she were present in the studio. The three-dimensional image of the journalist carried on a conversation with him, even though she was actually in Chicago.[2,3]

This technology was used when Prince Charles gave a speech in Abu Dubai at the World Future Energy Summit. The speech was recorded in the United Kingdom and shown at the summit, but Prince Charles wasn't actually there. However, holographic technology was used to create a virtual, three-dimensional image that talked to those present at the summit.[4]

Telstra, an Australian company, used a hologram in 2008 to beam its chief technology officer from Melbourne to a business meeting over four hundred miles away. Cisco Systems also uses this technology in their demonstrations when they talk about their telepresence products, although they do not transmit holographic images.

Through transmission of holographic images, a person can appear to be in multiple locations at one time. As technology has advanced, the hologram is so real that it can be difficult to look at two people standing on a stage together and tell which is real and which is a hologram.

Like all technology, there are benefits to using it. Taking digital photographs of yourself giving a speech and transmitting your three-dimensional figure hundreds or thousands of miles away to speak at a meeting would certainly save a lot of money on gas and travel expenses. As technology improves, new and better uses are always discovered for it. Could this holographic technology be used in the future to beam speeches by the Antichrist across the world, where his three-dimensional image could be seen and worshipped by people in the comfort of their own homes?

The Seal of Satan

The image of the beast, in whatever form it takes, will initiate the seal of Satan. This image is the "abomination that causes desolation" that was predicted by Daniel 2,500 years ago, when he penned the primary verse that deals with the seven-year tribulation and the Antichrist breaking the agreement and causing desolation in Jerusalem:

"He will confirm a covenant with many for one 'seven.' In the middle of the 'seven' he will put an end to sacrifice and offering. And on a wing [of the temple] he will set up an abomination that causes desolation, until the end that is decreed is poured out on him."

- Daniel 9:27 (NIV)

This prediction by Daniel was recognized centuries later during the writing of the New Testament, when Jesus spoke about the signs of His coming. In Matthew 24:14, Christ spoke of the gospel being preached and the end coming. He predicted that an abomination would occur in Jerusalem:

"When ye therefore shall see the abomination of desolation, spoken of by Daniel the prophet, stand in the holy place, (whoever reads, let him understand)..."

- Matthew 24:15 (KJV)

Notice the parenthesis, indicating that Matthew admitted he was uncertain of the meaning of Daniel's prophecy of the abomination. Matthew's gospel was written around 50 A.D., while the revelation of the meaning of "image of the beast" was not given to John until 95 A.D., over forty-five years after Matthew recorded his gospel. Both Daniel and Matthew had no full understanding of this abomination. However, the Law of Moses reveals that idolatry and idol worship is classified an abomination (Deut. 7:25-26; 12:29-31; 13:12-17). Many commentaries indicate that the primary meaning of an abomination is idolatry or idol worship.

The Hebrew text of Daniel's prophecy teaches that in the middle of the seven (the seven-year tribulation), an abomination will be set up, as it reads in Hebrew, on the "wing of the Temple" (Daniel 9:27). This could refer to the corner of a new Temple structure yet to be built, or it might have reference to the southeastern corner of the present wall of the Temple Mount, known as the pinnacle of the Temple. From either vantage point, thousands of people could visibly see the image and watch as the false prophet performs his false miracles.I can picture the image of the beast being positioned on the wing of the Temple for worshipers to see. Suddenly this icon will begin to move and speak in the sight of men. Multitudes will be deceived into believing that Christ himself has now returned to Jerusalem and is manifesting His presence for the world to see.

This would also fulfill the ancient expectations of the Islamic religion, which teaches that Jesus (Isa) will appear in Jerusalem and deny that He was God's Son. This "lamb with two horns" will effectively pull apostate Christians as well as Muslims (two horns) into his grasp, by denying the *deity* of Christ, by persecuting Jews, and by killing anyone who will not worship the image of the beast. All of this will play into the hands of Muslims throughout the world.

"And he had power to give life unto the image of the beast, that the image of the beast should both speak, and cause that as many as would not worship the image of the beast should be killed."

- Revelation 13:15

Death for non-worshipers will come by beheading (Rev.20:4), which is the 1,400-year-old method used in strict Islamic nations for capital crimes against the government or against Islam. This Islamic link to many troublesome prophecies related to the tribulation is undeniable.

The mark of the beast is a seal of Satan. A person will be unable to buy or sell without the mark, the name, or the number of this beast. The mark is on the right hand or forehead, and it could come in the form of a mark, a number, or a name. Numbers are used as personal identification to gain access to computers and data bases, and we have already explained that the current microchip designed for human implantation holds a 16-digit number, seven more digits than the social security numbers.

There is nothing evil about the use of numbers, computers, the Internet, or modern technology. We use technology in our daily lives, and most of the time, we are thankful for it. The issue is not the numbers; it is the fact that the Antichrist will lead a false religion, and the false prophet will help initiate the mark of the beast and demand worship of the beast and his image. They will succeed by tying their religion into complete control of the economic system of buying and selling. Similar circumstances exist today in strict Islamic-controlled countries, where the government, religion, and economic system are tied together inseparably. No other religion is permitted in those countries, and people who attempt to follow other religions are punished economically, tortured, or even killed.

The seal on the foreheads of the 144,000 is the seal of God. Conversely, on the seven heads of the beast are names full of blasphemy (Rev. 13:1, 6; 17:3). In this instance, a name or names of blasphemy would be the beast system blaspheming God and His name. In Revelation, God rebuked individuals who said they were Jews, but were of the synagogue of Satan. Christ said they were blaspheming (Rev. 2:9). To blaspheme would be to claim that a false god is the true God, and to deny the name and power of the One True God. A false Christ who claims to be the true Christ would be a blasphemer. Denying that Jesus Christ is the Son of God is the spirit of antichrist (1 John 2:18, 22; 4:3).

Those who resist the beast system and his image and mark will be killed for their resistance (Rev. 20:4). Why would God allow these people to perish for their firm stand against the lie and deceit, and allow others to receive the mark and appear to go unpunished? Again, these people who take the mark are committing themselves to a deceptive, lying, counterfeit system that is not just an economic system, but a system of false worship set up by Satan himself. It is Satan that gives his throne and dominion to the beast:

> *"Now the beast which I saw was like a leopard, his feet were like the feet of a bear, and his mouth like the mouth of a lion. The dragon gave him his power, his throne, and great authority."*
>
> - Rev. 13:2 (NKJV)

The tribulation will be time of trouble unlike any in the history of the world (Dan. 12:1), with plagues, judgments, and wars that could destroy all flesh without intervention from Christ (Matt. 24:22). Why? Because for forty-two months, Satan himself is in charge. This evil agent will be cast out of heaven in the middle of the seven years and go forth with great wrath (Rev. 12:7-10). Satan's nature is to kill, steal, and destroy (John 10:10). Paul wrote about the man of sin (the Antichrist) and said that his coming was after the working of Satan, with all power, signs, and lying wonders (2 Thess. 2:9). Those who follow him love not the truth (2 Thess. 2:10).

Satan has always desired to be like God (Isa. 14:14) and has always desired that people worship him. During those forty-two months Satan will receive, through the Antichrist, what he has longed for. Then the true King of kings will return, bind Satan, and cast the beast and the false prophet into the lake of fire (Rev. 19:20; 20:2).

If we assume, and the evidence seems to indicate, that the Antichrist is from the Middle East and has an Islamic background, then how might Islam play into the revelation of the number 666 and the mark of the beast?

CHAPTER 7

The Mark and the Symbols – an Islamic View

The primary verse that reveals the number of the beast is Revelation 13:18. Below are different translations of the same verse:

"Here is wisdom. Let him that hath understanding count the number of the beast: for it is the number of a man; and his number is six hundred threescore and six."

-Rev. 13:18 (KJV)

"Here is [room for] discernment [a call for the wisdom of interpretation]. Let anyone who has intelligence (penetration and insight enough) calculate the number of the beast, for it is a human number [the number of a certain man]; his number is 666."

- Rev. 13:18 (AMP)

"This calls for wisdom: let him who has understanding reckon the number of the beast, for it is a human number, its number is six hundred and sixty-six."

- Rev. 13:18 (RSV)

"Here is wisdom. Let him who has understanding calculate the number of the beast, for the number is that of a man; and his number is six hundred sixty-six."

-Rev. 13:18 (NASB)

"Here is a puzzle that calls for careful thought to solve it. Let those who are able, interpret this code: the numerical values of the letters in his name add to 666!"

- Rev. 13:18 (TLB)

Since the second century, early church fathers, Bible scholars, and students of prophecy have pored over this verse, dissected the words, and compared verses as they attempted to unlock the mysterious mark of the beast and the calculation of the number of his name. The lack of understanding throughout church history is evident when reading their commentaries:

"Despite numerous attempts to identify the mark of the beast with names, computers, monetary systems and the like, its precise nature is unknown, remaining to be disclosed as the end draws near."

- Merrill Unger

"I confess my ignorance as to the number six hundred and sixty-six. I cannot present you with anything satisfactory to myself. We find, answering to the number six hundred sixty six, the words apostasy and tradition: but I cannot say anything positive at this point."

- John Darby

"Irenaeus has only uncertain guesses to offer, and he thinks the Apocalypist intended the name remain hidden till the Antichrist should come. The language, however, implies that it is discoverable by those who have the requisite wisdom; and the command, let him that hath understanding calculate the number, shows that the author expects some to solve the enigma."

- Isbon Beckworth

"It seems to me to be one of those seasons which God has reserved in his own power; only this we know, God has written Mene Tekel upon all his enemies; he has numbered their days, and they shall be finished, but his own kingdom shall endure for ever."

- Matthew Henry's Commentary

One of the greatest prophetic mysteries throughout church history has been the meaning of the numbers six hundred sixty and six. When these numbers are transitioned into the value of Greek letters, they become chi, xi, and stigma, whose value is 600, 60, and 6. An older Christian commentary makes this statement:

"The common Greek text, it is expressed by the characters [ch] [x] [s] = 666. There can be no doubt that this is the correct number, though, in the time of Irenaeus, there was in some copies another reading—[ch] [i] [s] = 616. This reading was adopted by the expositor Tychonius; but against this Irenaeus inveighs (Liv. v.100:30). There can be no doubt that the number 666 is the correct reading, though it would seem that this was sometimes expressed in letters, and sometimes written in full. Wetstein supposes that both methods were used by John; that in the first copy of his book he used the letters, and in a subsequent copy wrote it in full."

- Barnes Notes on Revelation 13

The commentary reveals that in the text the actual Greek letters were used—chi, xi, and stigma, and it was also copied in the form of counting the letters as six hundred, sixty, and six. In most of today's translations of the Holy Scriptures, the 666 is spelled out with six hundred, threescore and six. However, in some of the oldest manuscripts of the New Testament, the 666 was identified by the three Greek letters.

All manuscripts of the Greek New Testament were copied by hand before the middle of the 15th century. Two Greek New Testaments from which modern versions are based are the *Textus Receptus* compiled by Erasmus in 1516 and the *Novum Testamentum Graece*, edited by Eberhardt Nestle in 1898.

Different Translations

Erasmus (1516) relied on twelfth and thirteenth century manuscripts which represented the Byzantine text, the Koine text, or the Majority text. For three hundred years the *Textus Receptus* remained the primary New Testament text. It is the text used by the 1611 King James translators of the Bible who translated the first English Bible that was approved by the King. The early fathers quoted from the Greek New Testament and we know the name as the *Textus Receptus*. Scholars knew this text as the Byzantine text and it was the main text read and used before the 1900s.

"The Majority Text, upon which the KJV is based, has in reality the strongest claim possible to be regarded as an authentic representation of the original text."

- Zane Hodges, Former Professor of Greek
Dallas Theological Seminary

In this old manuscript, the mark of the beast is identified by the three Greek letters—chi, xi, and stigma—rather than by the numbers, 666. These three letters are found in the third century Egyptian text and in the Majority text. It was in the later 1800s that Nestle, instead of using these three letters, added up the numerical value of these letters to 666.

From the Greek Interlinear Bible

As a reminder, the reason they used for doing this was because the number six hundred, sixty, and six (666) is the gematria of the three Greek letters. The Greek letter chi has a number value of 600; the letter xi has a value of 60; and the letter stigma has a value of 6. Thus the three Greek letters had a numerical value of six hundred, sixty, and six.

Greek Letters Representing "666" (Revelation 13:18–Byzantine Text)		
X	ξ	ς
CHI	XI	STIGMA
600	60	6

The Letter Chi

The Greek letter chi has a form similar to the Ancient Hebrew letter taw (or tav in Modern Hebrew), which is the twenty-second and final letter of the Hebrew alphabet. The Ancient Hebrew letter taw was different in form from the Modern Hebrew letter tav. The Greek letter chi appears as an x, and the Ancient Hebrew form of taw was also + or x. The pictograph assigned to the Hebrew letter taw was crossed sticks, and one of the meanings of the word is "mark."[1]

In Greek, the name Christ begins with the letter chi (x). In the early Roman church the Greek letters chi and rho were the mark or monogram of Christian Rome. Chi has a numerical value of six hundred.

The Letter Xi

The second Greek letter found in the Revelation manuscript is xi. The numerical value of this Greek letter is 60.

The Greek letter for xi is similar to the Ancient Hebrew letter sin, which in Modern Hebrew is the letter samech. This is the fifteenth letter of the Hebrew alphabet, and like other Hebrew letters, the ancient letter differs in appearance from the modern letter. In Ancient Hebrew, the pictograph assigned to the letter sin was "thorn," and the meaning was pierce, sharp, protect, or grab.[2]

The Letter Stigma

There are twenty-four letters in the Greek alphabet, plus some archaic letters. In ancient times the archaic Greek letter digamma represented the "w" sound, but it fell into disuse and was later supplanted by stigma and used as a symbol for the number six. In the Modern Greek alphabet, stigma has been replaced by sigma.

This Greek letter is similar in appearance to the Ancient Hebrew letter shin, which is the twenty-first letter of the Hebrew alphabet. When shin is used as a prefix in Hebrew, it bears the same meaning as "that, which, or who." In Hebrew, the word also stands for Shaddai, which is a name for God.

Both the Hebrew and Greek alphabets interchange the letters of the alphabet with numbers. In the Hebrew tradition, one of the thirty-two laws of hermeneutics is called gematria. In gematria, a letter can be exchanged for a number, entire words can be added up to equal a numerical value, and entire sentences can be added up to find mysteries hidden in the Biblical text. Let's examine the numbers for the Greek letters chi (600), xi (60), and stigma (6).

The Number 666

Through the centuries, students of the Bible have concentrated on the number 666. Using the concept of exchanging letters for numbers, scholars and students throughout the centuries have attempted to calculate the names of world leaders, dictators, and religious leaders whose names might add up to 666.

The first person in early church history to have been considered a candidate for the Antichrist was Nero. Other scholars have attempted to identify Judas Iscariot as the future Antichrist, noting that the Antichrist is identified as the "son of perdition," a title that was also given to Judas (John 17:12; 2 Thess. 2:3). A few Greek scholars such as Kenneth Weust, in his book *Prophetic Light in Present Darkness,* have taken this as a cryptic clue, identifying Judas Iscariot as the son of perdition who will arise from the pit of hell, return to earth during the tribulation, take possession of a human body (the embodiment of evil), and thus become the Antichrist.

From the time of the apocalypse to the present, centuries have passed and global political and military leaders such as Napoleon, Hitler, Kissinger, and President Bill Clinton's names were added up to a calculation of 666 using various alphabets and numerical codes. Some said President Ronald Wilson Reagan was the Antichrist because his names had six letters each—six, six, six. Needless to say, this numerology did nothing to help spread the prophetic message or to prove anything, other than to spark a temporary fire of sensationalism.

The fact is that nobody has been able to give a clear, solid understanding of the true prophetic meaning of these three Greek letters, and how they will fit into the name, number, or mark of the beast. But let's explore some unusual possibilities that have been discussed in recent years.

Could the Letters be Symbols?

All twenty-two letters of the Hebrew alphabet are not only used to form words, but each letter has a symbol that it represents. I have already mentioned, for example, that the picture symbol for tav is crossed sticks. The reason for the symbols is that, before the alphabet took on the form of letters, it was first in the form of symbols or word pictures, in the same manner of hieroglyphics. These pictures were "read" to reveal a message.

Is it possible that the letters chi, xi, and stigma are hidden clues that give us more insight into the future beast and his religion?

The Greek letter chi has the appearance of the English letter x. In Greek, this letter is the first of two letters in the Greek word Christos, a Greek word given to Christ, the Anointed One.

Former Muslim Walid Shoebat made an observation about the Greek letters chi, xi, and stigma. He said the Greek letters bore a striking resemblance to Arabic letters, which are read right to left instead of left to right. Using this right to left format, the first letter read would be stigma. He noted that in Arabic, this letter reads "in the name of."

The second letter used in Revelation 13:18 is the Greek letter xi. Shoebat noted that this letter is very similar in appearance to the Arabic letters that form the name Allah. We see that, from right to left, the combination of stigma and xi in Greek read "in the name of Allah" in Arabic.

Allah is the name that Muslims use for God, and all Muslims claim that he is the same god who is worshiped by Jews and Christians. However, scholars note that the name Allah was actually the name of a moon deity that was worshiped in pre Islamic times among the Arabs throughout the Arabian Peninsula. Even the Hindus consider the crescent moon to be a symbol of two of their primary gods, Shiva and Parvati. Hindus also claim that the Islamic ka'aba in Mecca dates back to pre-Islamic times and was originally a Hindu temple of Shiva.[3] Archaeology seems to indicate that these two cultures were once linked.

Some scholars allege that Muhammad may have used the name Allah to help win many of the tribal people who had been involved in the worship of the moon prior to the time of Muhammad's revelations. Notice that the crescent moon is placed on mosques, and the crescent is also a symbol used on the flags of several Islamic nations.

As another point of interest, this Greek letter xi is also similar to the Hindu symbol for the word "om." This word is an important part of all Hindu mantras because they teach that it is the breath of the universe that first sounded during creation. The believe "om" is the most suitable name for god.[4]

The next Greek letter, chi, is in the form of an x. Interestingly, the Saudi Arabian civil ensign is a sword, and sometimes two swords that cross one another in the shape of an x. Saudi Arabia is the most important nation on earth for the Islamic religion. This is where Islam's prophet Muhammad received his "revelations" that formed the contents of their religious book called the Qur'an, and thus it is where the Islamic religion began. Saudi Arabia is also the land of Islam's two most important cities, Mecca and Medina, and it is the world headquarters for all Muslims. Today, Muslims say that Jerusalem is also an important city for Islam, but Jerusalem is never mentioned in the Qur'an.

Mecca is home to the famous ka'aba, the ancient stone draped with a black cloth and covered with verses from the Qur'an. The ka'aba is located inside the grand mosque in Mecca, where millions of Muslims each year perform the hajj (pilgrimage). Medina is the city where Mohammad is buried. Saudi Arabia is such a strict Islamic nation that the practice of any other religion is forbidden. To proselytize or practice any form of religion other than Islam is punishable by prison or death. Some crimes are punished by beheading, which is permissible in certain circumstances according by the Qur'an.

The Lamb with the Mark

The definition of the word stigma is a mark. The word mark, as used in the book of Revelation, is *charagma*, and it means mark, stamp, image, or idol. It can be an actual spot or scar; a mark of shame or discredit; an identifying mark or characteristic; or some indication of idol worship. In years past, a stigma was a mark or a tattoo that was used to brand or identify slaves and criminals. These marks were also used as a rite of passage, such as within a tribe, or to signify membership in an organization.

Throughout history, slaves were marked by slaveholders to indicate ownership. In Ancient Rome, new slave recruits to gladiator schools had Roman tattoos applied as an identifying mark on their face, legs, and hands. In the 16th century, German Anabaptists were branded with a cross on their foreheads for refusing to recant their faith and join the Roman Catholic Church. And in the 17th century Puritan settlements, adulterers were branded with the letter "A."

In 2002, an unusual lamb was born in Durmen Village, Uzbekistan, just three days before a major Islamic holiday called Eid-al-Adha, or feast of the sacrifice. This feast marks the end of Islam's annual pilgrimage to Mecca and Medina.[5]

The lamb caused quite a stir because it was born with unusual markings. On the dark fleece of the lamb was a white pattern that formed the Arabic words for Allah on one side and Muhammad on the other side. Muslims called it the "lamb of Allah," believing it was sent by Allah to strengthen their faith.

In 2004, Palestinians in Israel flocked to see another such lamb that was born in Hebron, on the same day that militant leader, Sheikh Ahmed Yassin, was killed. Again, it was born with the Arabic symbol for Allah on the side of its body.[6]

I realize that this approach of using Greek letters as symbols to represent a name or a religion is controversial and much different from the traditional interpretation of the 666 prophecy. While most traditional teachers and students of prophecy will not accept this interpretation, it still might be a clue to indicate the Islamic influence and the strategy to use the religion and its followers to control much of the Middle East, Europe, and even the rest of the world.

If the Antichrist is indeed a Muslim, he would be a follower of Muhammad and would believe that he is the final and true prophet. He would believe and teach that the Qur'an is the only true and final word of God on earth, and he would refer to his god as Allah, never using the Hebrew names for God as recorded in the Scriptures. How might the number six be linked to Islam?

The Number Six

Numbers in the Bible carry significance, and oftentimes they carry a meaning. For example, we see the number three associated with units, such as faith, hope, and love (1 Cor. 13:13); body, soul, and spirit (1 Thess. 5:23); and the Trinity—the Father, the Word (the Son), and the Holy Spirit (1 John 5:7).The word seven is found 463 times in the Bible. The number seven alludes to fullness and completion, and is often identified with some form of perfection. Seven has been called "God's perfect number." Other numbers, such as twelve, allude to government and divine order. There were twelve tribes of Israel, twelve disciples, and twenty-four elders (twelve times two).

The number six is recognized as the number of man. God formed man on the sixth day of creation (Gen. 1:27-31). Man was given six days to work and was to rest on the seventh (Exod. 20:9-10). Goliath, the giant from Gath, was six cubits and a span, with a description of six weapons, including the head of his spear which weighed six hundred shekels of iron (1 Samuel 17:4-7). The image set up by Nebuchadnezzar in Babylon, which was a picture of the future image of the beast, was sixty cubits high and the breadth was six cubits.

The number six is seen in the Islamic religion; for example: Mohammad was born in the year 622. Muslims worship on the sixth day of the week, which is on Friday (Saturday being the seventh day), and the Qur'an has a total of 6,666 verses. One Muslim even declares on his website:

"The number 666 is highly publicized all over the world and it is associated with danger. However, it is not what it seems. It was a satanic trick. The trick was to prevent the people approaching 666. Satan knew that the 666 is the book of god and the people should be kept away from it. According to his plan, he placed a bad image to the number 666."[7]

The predominant religions are centered on certain religious figures. Christianity is centered on Christ, Islam is centered on Mohammad, and Judaism on patriarchs such as Abraham and Moses. But Christianity is the only religion whose message can be demonstrated with signs, wonders, miracles, and deliverance (Heb. 2:4). However, in the final years of the tribulation, a series of dramatic counterfeit miracles, such as fire falling from heaven and an image that lives, will turn the masses into followers of the beast and his religious companion. The nations surrounding Israel and those involved in the time of the end are Islamic nations. However, there will be non-Islamic nations involved in the time of the end, including a coalition called the "kings of the east" (Rev. 16:12). Is it possible that some of the symbolism used in the apocalyptic literature could have a double meaning? We have already seen possible dual meanings, and perhaps there is additional prophetic symbolism that is a clue to another empire.

CHAPTER 8

Red Dragon Rising – The Coming Mr. Xi

"And another sign appeared in heaven: behold, a great, fiery red dragon having seven heads and ten horns, and seven diadems on his heads. His tail drew a third of the stars of heaven and threw them to the earth..."
— Rev. 12:3-4 (NKJV)

The biblical books of Daniel and Revelation are filled with apocalyptic symbolism. Ancient symbolism was used to identify nations and even certain world leaders, both past and future. In Daniel chapter 7, the prophet identified major prophetic empires as a lion (Babylon), a bear (Media-Persia), and a leopard (Greece).

In John's vision, he saw a beast rise up out of the sea, which was a combination of all three of these animals on one body. He saw the body of a leopard, with feet of a bear, and mouth like a lion (Rev. 13:1 2). These three empires—Babylon, Media-Persia, and Greece—primarily covered the land masses that are now Egypt, Libya, Ethiopia, Israel, Jordan, Lebanon, Syria, Iraq, Iran, Afghanistan, Pakistan, and areas of Greece and Turkey.

Some scholars have noted that in Daniel chapter 7, these three animal kingdoms of the lion, the bear, and the leopard also have a parallel with the symbols of certain nations today. For example, the British emblem is a lion.

In Daniel 7, there are two wings of an eagle that are plucked off the lion's back. The lion was made to stand like a man, and a man's heart was given to him (Dan. 7:4). America began as a British colony but separated from the lion of Britain and stood alone as a nation among nations.

Eventually, the next major empire to impact the world was the Soviet Union, whose revolution in 1917 introduced Communism to the world. The bear became a symbol of Russia and the Soviet empire. Following the bear was the leopard, which has been linked by some to Nazi Germany and the Third Reich.

One of the apocalyptic symbols in Revelation is a great red dragon with seven heads and ten horns (Rev. 12:3). The word dragon appears several times in the book of Revelation (Rev. 12:3-4, 7, 9, 13, 16-17; 13:2, 4, 11; 16:13; 20:2). The word actually refers to a large serpent, perhaps similar to a huge anaconda. But this serpent has seven heads and is identified as Satan himself (Rev. 12). In ancient cultures, the dragon was thought to dwell in waste places and in wilderness areas (Isa. 13:22).

Adam Clark, according to his commentary, believed this dragon was an emblem of pagan Rome. He noted that, according to ancient writers, the dragon standards of the Romans were painted red. The first standard of the entire Roman legion was the eagle, the standard and traditional emblem of Imperial Rome. Later dragon symbols were brought into the battle.[1] The red dragon emblem is interesting, especially as it relates to China. This powerful nation, in the time of the end, seems to be rising like a flooded river. China is often associated with a red dragon.

China and the Kings of the East

The dragon is a legendary creature found in mythology and folklore of many East Asian countries, including China, Japan, Korea, and Vietnam.

The Bible tells us that a coalition of the "kings of the east" will unite an army and march from the east toward the Middle Eastern nation of Iraq, crossing the dried Euphrates River and bringing an army of "two hundred thousand thousand," which totals two hundred million (Rev. 9:14-16; 16:12-16). An army this size has never been united in the history of the world. Even in John's day, there might have been a total of one hundred million men in the entire Roman Empire.

The Chinese have a population of over 1.3 billion; and with a world population of over 6.7 billion, this means that China has almost twenty percent of the world's population under their control.

China also has a law which limits the number of children to one per household, which is especially enforced in poor families. Daughters are often aborted because it is more desirable to have a son who can carry on the family name, provide for the family, and lead in ancestor worship. There are 119 boys for every 100 girls born in China. By 2020, there could be thirty to forty million more boys than girls in China.

A male population of this size could create a sizeable army. These kings of the east will be marching for war, and some suggest they will be present at the battle of Armageddon (Rev. 16:16).

The Chinese Dragon

The emblem of a dragon being linked with China possibly began with the Emperor of China during the Yaun dynasty, which ended around the year 1368. In Chinese imagery the dragon is a snake-like creature with large scales and four claws. They believe that a dragon symbolizes power, control, strength, and good luck. In the 1970s, the term "descendents of the dragon" was used by many Chinese people as their animal symbol.

They also believe it is associated with weather and rain, which is interesting considering the symbolism in Revelation chapter 12. In the narrative, the dragon spews water from its mouth to cause a flood against the remnant of the Jews dwelling in the wilderness.

China, part of the Ancient Orient, is located in an area of the world identified for centuries as the Far East. The Biblical phrase, "kings of the east," is interesting when we consider the word east in this context. The Greek word is *anatole* and, besides being one of the four directions on a compass, it also refers to *rising light* or *the dawn*. It is a word used for sunlight. The name Japan in Japanese is Nippon or Nihon and literally means "the sun's origin." The flag of Japan has a white background with a large red disk that represents the sun, which is called in Japanese, nisshoki. The lands of the Far East, which include China, Japan, Vietnam, and Korea, are possibly areas from where the kings of the east will make their trek to the Middle East.

One critic wrote to me and said, "How is this possible when there are no roads and only massive mountains separating the area?" The answer would simply be the Silk Road, an ancient seven-thousand-mile trade route connecting China with countries all the way to the Mediterranean Sea. The road spans two continents. While this is an ancient trade road, it has been used again in recent years. A gentleman from Pakistan sent me information that included news articles about a major road that China was building that was sizeable enough to haul large pieces of military equipment and a massive number of people. The road was leading right into the Middle East.

China is supportive of Islamic nations and provides them with military equipment. When this book was being written, Israeli newspapers reported that the U.S. State Department was aware that a Chinese company was involved in the transfer of equipment and technology to Iran for the development of their chemical weapons program. In 2007, this particular Chinese company was blacklisted by America amid suspicions that they supplied similar equipment to Iran, North Korea, and Syria.

China's support of these Middle Eastern nations is not based on religion, but upon oil and gas that is available to them through these countries. Iran is the fifth largest exporter of oil, most of which is sold to Asian countries. Right now, China is growing so fast that, in the years to come, they will see a massive increase in their need for oil. China's demand for energy is expected to increase 150% by the year 2020. By 2030, China will need the same amount of oil that is now being consumed in the United States. At this time, the U.S. uses over eighteen million barrels of oil a day, almost nine million of which is consumed by motor vehicles.[2]

News outlets also have reported on China's successful attempts at espionage against the United States. Chinese intelligence officers recruit spies—generally Americans—who land jobs with manufacturers or U.S. government agencies such as the State Department or even the CIA. As of this writing, at least fifty-seven defendants have been involved in federal prosecutions since 2008, all charged in espionage conspiracies with China.

Spies have passed classified information, sensitive technology, and trade secrets to Chinese operatives, state-sponsored entities, private individuals, or Chinese businesses. Some of our most sensitive military information related to such things as the design of cruise missiles, nuclear-powered subs, and the space shuttle has been passed to China. Parts for military radar and electronic warfare systems have been sold to Chinese research institutes and manufacturers. Beijing denies that espionage is happening, but U.S. counterintelligence experts say the threat is real, it is growing, and the Chinese are changing tactics as they become bolder in their efforts.

Coalition Fighting Coalition

The nations of the world will eventually form coalitions based upon regions, religion, and ethnic groups. They will do this for survival. The Antichrist will have his unit of ten kings under his control, while the kings of the east are an Asian coalition. The European Union currently has twenty-seven member nations with more planning to join, uniting with one currency, one passport, and a unit without borders for trade. There are discussions of a western coalition, called the North American Union, which is a merger of America, Canada, and Mexico.

Once the Antichrist forges his coalition of ten kings, he will become "great toward the south, and toward the east and toward the Pleasant Land" (Dan. 8:9). There are several Islamic nations east of Israel, including Jordan, Iraq, Iran, Afghanistan, and Pakistan. However, to the far east of Israel are China, Japan, Vietnam, and Korea. When the Antichrist seizes Egypt, Libya and Ethiopia, we read that "news from the east and the north shall trouble him" (Dan. 11:43-44). Eventually, the "kings of the east" will march across the dry river bed of the once-productive Euphrates River to head to the land of the beast and prepare for the battle of Armageddon (Rev. 16:16).

In apocalyptic symbolism, the meaning of the dragon is explained in the Scripture:

> *"So the great dragon was cast out, that serpent of old, called the Devil and Satan, who deceives the whole world; he was cast to the earth, and his angels were cast out with him."*
>
> - Rev. 12:9 – NKJV

China is a communist country, and the color red has been associated with communism. When Joseph Stalin came to power, he purged the government of all parties other than his own, and he identified his party as the "Red Guard." The flag of the former Soviet Union was a hammer and sickle on a red background, and during World War II, their soldiers were identified by red bands on their right arms. In China, the propaganda book handed out to the youth to promote communism was called the "red book."

Early in the tribulation there is a red horse rider that takes peace from the earth, killing with a great sword (Rev. 6:4). Because communism is identified with the color red, and this red horse rider takes peace and uses a sword (war), some suggest this is an imagery of communist nations that will rise again, initiating war and death.

I have heard ministers say that communism has collapsed. But in reality, the communist Chinese government is one of the world's greatest abusers of human rights and a great persecutor of citizens who stand in opposition to the government. The nations of Vietnam and North Korea are also communist strongholds. Even after the dissolution of the USSR and the fall of communism in the Eastern Bloc European nations, the East Asian region remained under communist rule.

This great dragon (Satan) of the apocalypse is red. Why red, and not white, green, black, yellow, or some other color? In the Bible colors have meanings. For example, white normally signifies righteousness, and purple is kingly. Red (or scarlet) often is a picture of the blood, redemption, or the covenant; for example, Rahab placed a scarlet cord in the window and was spared from destruction at Jericho (Joshua 2:21). Red can allude to Satan's great anger and wrath (Rev. 12:12). In ancient times, some nations saw the color red as representative of fire.

Consider the numbers of people slain under communist dictators. Out of sixty-one million people killed in the Soviet Union by communists, Joseph Stalin was responsible for killing forty-three million of them, with thirty-nine million dying in gulags (labor camps) or in transit.

An estimated one million people have been murdered in China under various regimes, and countless thousands have been slain in Vietnam, Cambodia, and Korea. Estimates indicate that communists have killed about 110 million people from 1900 to the present. Since the dragon, or Satan, is identified with the color red, it is clear that communism was and still is one of the belief systems of the dragon.

In light of this, and considering that one of the Greek letters of the beast is xi, here is an interesting fact connected with the name Xi.

The Man Named Xi

Just as the animal symbolism marking ancient empires can have certain parallels among contemporary nations, we also find that the Scripture alludes to names that are prophetic. In reality, they might have little bearing on actual prophetic fulfillment, but they are interesting, nonetheless.

For example, the days of Noah will be repeated before the return of Christ (Matt. 24:37-38). This includes eating, drinking, marrying, building, planting, and giving in marriage (Matt. 24:38; Luke 17:27-28). Other insights concerning the parallels are concealed in the story of Noah and the flood. We are told that violence filled the earth (Gen. 6:11). The Hebrew word violence is *chamac*, and the root word is the word is *hamas*. Today the name Hamas is the name of the political and military wing of the fanatical Islamic organization that is continually initiating violence against Israel and the Jews who live there!

The prophet Zechariah saw a vision of a women being carried in a lead basket to the plains of Shinar, the land of the ancient tower of Babel (Gen. 11) and the location of Nebuchadnezzar's Babylon (Dan. 1:1-2). This woman in the basket is called "wickedness" (Zech 5:8). We read:

> *"So I said to the angel who talked with me, 'Where are they carrying the basket?' And he said to me, 'To build a house for it in the land of Shinar; when it is ready, the basket will be set there on its base.' "*
>
> - Zech. 5:10-11 NKJV

There will be a house of wickedness in the future in Shinar—the land known today as Iraq. In apocalyptic literature, a woman such as the harlot in Revelation 17 can often refer to a counterfeit religious system or a false religion. The wickedness will be set in a base. In this passage, the Hebrew word base is *mekunah*, and refers to a specific location.

After more than a decade of research and study, I have concluded that the Antichrist will have an Islamic background and will rise from the Middle East. Islamic tradition places the appearance of their awaited one (the Mahdi) in Iraq—in either the city of Karbala or the city of Samarra (depending upon the Sunni or Shiite traditions). Since this final dictator will behead resisters (Rev. 20:4) and use a sword to conquer, he will gain millions of Islamic followers that are classified as fanatics.

One such Islamic organization that has global exposure and just won't go away is Al-Qaeda. Even though Osama bin Laden is now dead, other fanatical leaders have and will continue to step into his place. This group of terrorists and fanatics is scattered throughout nations in and around the Mediterranean. Ironically, the name Al-Qaeda means, "the base."

Wickedness personified will be set on a base, according to Zechariah, and Al Qaeda means "the base!"

While Ad-Qaeda is perhaps the most well-known among the terrorist groups, there are many other Islamic terrorist groups that exist throughout the world. One of the Shiite clerics who returned from Iraq after being exiled in Iran is Muqtada Al-Sadr, the founder and head of a large militia organization of Shiite Muslims called the Mahdi army. This group is headquartered in Iraq.

In the book of Ezekiel, we read of a coalition of Islamic nations that invade Israel in a war that, according to Jewish Rabbi's, Muslims and Christians, is the battle indicating the time of the end. The prophet announced that the Lord was against "Gog, the land of Magog, the chief prince of Meshech and Tubal" (Ezek. 38:2-3).

Who or what is Gog? In the Eastern European nations, including the Russian confederation, there are men whose surname is Gog. The word Gog also could be the name of a strong demonic prince spirit (Eph. 6:12) that rules over the region north of Israel. It could even be the name of a commander that will direct the battle, leading the Islamic hordes with a northern coalition.

This brings us back to the mark of the beast and the three Greek letters that are used to count the number of the beast. The second Greek letter is the letter xi, which has a numerical equivalency of 60. It is interesting that in China, Xi is also a surname (pronounced Shee). One such man, whom observers suggest will become the future leader of China, is named Xi Jinping. He currently serves as the country's Vice President, was appointed one of the Vice-Chairman of the Central Military Commission, and serves as a top-ranking member of the Secretariat of the Communist Party of China. He has a strong communist lineage and has worked his way up through party ranks.[3]

Mr. Xi is currently being groomed to be the nation's next President. It is presumed he will take over the leadership of China when the current leader steps down. The name Xi means sunrise in Chinese.

Notice the odd parallels. There is a dragon in Revelation, and the mythological dragon has been noted as an emblem of China and former Chinese dynasties. China remains a communist nation, and the color identifying communism is red—the same color as the second of the four horses of the Apocalypse—and the color of the great red dragon.

China, with over 1.3 billion people, is not only an aggressive and prosperous nation in economic growth and development, but will no doubt lead the kings of the east toward the land of the beast when they cross the Euphrates River toward Israel. Then we see that one of the numbers of the beast contains the Greek letter xi, which is the same name of a powerful leader in China. Economists and leaders say there is no question that China will take the place of the United States in military, technology, and economic power in time to come.

With the alignment of the nations and coalitions, and with advanced computer technology, revolutions in the Islamic world, economic debt, food shortages, and oil crises, the world is being set up for the man of sin who will set his throne among the world kingdoms and introduce his economic system based upon a new religion in which he attempts to make himself god.

The Bible tells us that Christ will appear and gather the family of God, both in heaven and in earth, unto himself when He descends with a shout, with the voice of an archangel, and with the trumpet of God (Eph. 1:9-10; 1 Thess. 4:16). The timing of this event is either before, in the middle of, or at the conclusion of the final seven-year tribulation. After much careful study, I tend to believe the gathering together for the overcoming church will happen before the man of sin is revealed, and before he signs the treaty of Daniel 9:27.

This does not mean, however, that the church will not see persecution. We will also witnesses prophetic events linked to natural disasters and selective judgments, as there are numerous birth pain signs that occur before the time of the end (Matt. 24:6-8). Considering the fact that a prudent person is to prepare if they see difficulties coming (Prov. 22:3), how should believers prepare for the times in which we live?

CHAPTER 9

Eight Suggestions for Preparing for the Last Days

Matthew 24 is a unique chapter which begins with Christ and His disciples viewing the magnificent Temple. As they boasted about the beauty of the structure, Christ suddenly predicted that the day would come when not one stone would be left upon another (Matt. 24:2). The disciples were interested in the signs leading up to the return of Christ and the end of the age (Matt. 24:3). Jesus gave them signs linked to events from the time of the destruction of the Temple, all the way up to the time He returns to set up His kingdom (Matt. 24:3-31). Christ gave instructions for the Jews living in Judea to "flee to the mountains," and if they were on the rooftops of their homes, not to go into the house and attempt to gather belongings, but to escape immediately (Matt. 24:16-18). Another gospel writer gave additional details about Christ's warnings when he wrote:

"When you see Jerusalem compassed with armies, then know that the desolation thereof is nigh"

- Luke 21:20

In Luke's narrative, he states that this is the time when those in Judea should flee to the mountains (Luke 21:21). At this time, according to Luke's account in verse 24, Jerusalem "will be trodden down of the Gentiles, until the times of the Gentiles be fulfilled," indicating that Gentile powers would seize Jerusalem until the fullness of time would come. Christ even wept over Jerusalem and said their judgment would come, as they were guilty of shedding the blood of the righteous, and their "house would be left desolate" (Matt. 23:37-38). Christ had predicted that these tragic events would come to pass on the generation to whom he was speaking (Matt. 24:34).

Believers Began Leaving the City

In the book of Acts, Luke reported that believers in the city began to sell their land and distribute the money to the poorer among them.

"And Joses, who was also named Barnabas by the apostles (which is translated Son of Encouragement), a Levite of the country of Cyprus, having land, sold it, and brought the money and laid it at the apostles' feet."
- Acts 4:36-37 (NKJV)

The very next verse introduces Acts 5:1, in which a couple named Ananias and Sapphira sold a possession and kept back kept back part of the proceeds (Acts 5:1). It appears that the selling of property or possessions was occurring primarily in Jerusalem. There is no indication that believers in other nations or cities were selling property and distributing the income among the poor. I have heard individuals use these verses to justify the political position of increasing taxes on the wealthy and engaging in redistribution of wealth. But further investigation will reveal why this was occurring. It was based upon the insight given by Christ Himself that Jerusalem would be left desolate.

If you knew, with a hundred percent accuracy, that the city in which you live would be destroyed and, in the process, you would lose your home and all of your possessions, how would you react or plan? This was the position of the believers living in Jerusalem. They knew that, within a generation, the Roman armies would surround the city, destroying both the Temple and the city.

I believe this is why these Christians sold their land and possessions, and assisted the poor with the proceeds. They knew it would do no good to continue to hold onto something that their family would lose in the future. What could they do with the land after the people were taken captive and scattered among the nations?

There is historical evidence that, prior to the destruction of the Temple, many Christians left the city and the regions around Judea, and fled to the country of Jordan to a place called Pella. Eusebius (325) wrote, "But the people of the church of Jerusalem had been commanded by a revelation, vouchsafed to approved men there before the war, to leave the city and to dwell in a certain town of Perea called Pella."[1] He wrote that those who left Jerusalem were believers in Christ.

Some historians teach that the believers were warned by an angel to leave the city, which is certainly possible. Historians indicate that all of Christ's followers fled prior to the destruction because of the warnings of Christ and of the pious religious men who discerned the warnings. By the time that Titus came to destroy Jerusalem, there was not a Christian left in the city! Christians who fled were spared the famine and destruction of Jerusalem. They were given asylum in Jordan where they built a great community of believers that existed for many generations. I share this as an important part of what I am preparing to tell you. There are parts of the world, including places within the United States, where there are serious warnings from geologists and scientists who have stated that, in the future, there will be either earthquakes or volcanic eruptions that will destroy entire cities and communities. Believers should pray and use spiritual discernment and the direction of the Holy Spirit to know whether they should relocate or remain in the area. Nobody except the Lord knows the exact timing of these events.

That being said, my recommendations concerning living in these times are simple and can be applied by everyone, regardless of where you live.

Suggestion 1 - Become as debt free as possible

We have all witnessed the difficulties that arise with unrestrained debt. In the days of my grandparents, people paid cash for everything, with the exception of a home or a car. However, when credit cards were issued, people found it easy to shop on credit, without ever considering interest rates and repayment. I have known individuals who had credit card debt of $50,000 to $100,000, and were caught in a web of paying monthly interest of over twenty-five percent. Those with high credit debt often pay only the minimum payment and never catch up.

There are two important Scriptures dealing with borrowing money:

"The rich ruleth over the poor, and the borrower is servant to the lender."

- Proverbs 22:7

"Owe no man anything, but to love one another: for he that loveth another hath fulfilled the law."

- Romans 13:8

While we will always have the basic monthly bills for food, utilities, gas for vehicles, insurance, clothing, taxes, and so forth, the largest bills that require borrowing are the home mortgage, car payments, and college loans. With economic uncertainty, it is important to cut your debt and exercise discretion in spending. Pay down debts, especially credit card debts with high interest.

In our culture today, it is almost impossible not to have a credit card. We travel continually and it is impossible to rent a car without a valid credit card. Hotels require a card on file for incidentals and even for reserving the room. If you travel, a credit card is a necessity. However, if a person cannot pay the charges in full each month, they should rethink the way they are using the card.

There is a mental and emotional freedom that comes with living a debt-free life. In our ministry, it costs millions of dollars each year to reach the world with the gospel through the seven-point outreach and the television ministry. We are also involved in world missions, which includes helping orphanages, feeding the poor and needy, and ministering to those in prison. Each month there are many expenses, including providing salaries for our employees and insurance for full-time workers.

However, all thanks to the Lord who has provided finances to do this, both of our buildings, the land, the television equipment, props, and the office equipment are debt free. We also arrange to pay our television air time for each station about twelve months in advance. This prevents me from being concerned about how we are going to meet the payments or bank loans each month. We choose not to make a purchase or build anything unless we can do so without taking a loan, as the borrower is a servant to the lender.

Being debt free also enables me to preach a direct message, even though at times it provokes people and they stop supporting the ministry. When a ministry owes huge debts, it can be tempting to water down the message to avoid offending individuals who help support the ministry. Being debt-free helps the minister continue moving forward with the work of the ministry, even though people say they will no longer support you because of what you are preaching.

Marriages are under stress, divorces are on the rise, and arguments are birthed by the pressure of massive debts. With the natural disasters and perilous times that are coming prior to the return of Christ, the more debt a person has, the more cares of life they will be under. Paul wrote:

"You therefore must endure hardship as a good soldier of Jesus Christ. No one engaged in warfare entangles himself with the affairs of this life, that he may please him who enlisted him as a soldier."
- 2 Tim. 2:3-4 (NKJV)

The word *entangleth* means to be encumbered, like a person wearing a heavy, long garment that their feet get tangled in, causing them to stumble.

Suggestion 2 - Become as independent as possible

Paul said that "Whatsoever state you are in, be content." The Greek word for content here actually means to "be sufficient in one's self," or to "be self sufficient and needing no assistance."[2] Paul was a full-time traveling evangelist and missionary who was dependent upon the free will offerings of the churches so he could travel and support the churches in need. However, there were times when he lacked needed funds and had to turn to a trade he was familiar with—tent making (Acts 18:1-3). He said, "We labor, working with our own hands" (1 Cor. 4:12).

Part of becoming independent involves learning to care for yourself physically. For some reason the traditional medical field seems to be less supportive of natural medicine, such as the use of vitamins, herbs, and other God-given health remedies. Before modern medicine, our ancestors had to use home and natural remedies, all of which were found within the earth. Many of these were not quack cures, but were proven remedies handed down from generation to generation. This is not to say that you should stop taking medicine you have been prescribed and are taking under a doctor's care; however, we should learn to take preventive care so that we are healthier and do not need so much prescribed medication.

With the rise in health costs and the possible cut backs in care, especially for the elderly, believers must learn to take better care of themselves. Many Christians would never smoke or drink alcohol, which is certainly a good thing for your health as well as your Christian testimony. But they will eat foods that clog their arteries, raise their blood pressure, and slowly damage their organs. If we can stay in better health, we can also keep from spending time and money on medical care. Don't be like the man who said, "If I had known I would live this long, I would have taken better care of myself."

The second recommendation is to become independent in your food supply. The prophecies indicate terrible food shortages as we approach the time of the end. Many of our ancestors were farmers who canned their food for the long winter. Today, most of us have no clue how to grow food and preserve it for difficult times. However, we should learn how and teach the younger generation.

My wife Pam grew a garden in bales of straw in the back yard where she planted tomatoes and other vegetable plants. (Small gardens can also be grown in plastic planting containers.) Later she expanded her little farm by planting eight kinds of vegetables on a small piece of property. It produced enough cucumbers, okra, and peppers that we were able to have food and give some away.

Then she bought everything she needed to can some of the food. I would come home from work and find Pam and several other ladies cutting beans or some other vegetable and canning them in glass jars. By the end of summer she had canned over 150 jars of food we had grown, sharing them with those who had worked on the "farm." During the winter months we ate beans, soup, okra, pickles, and other food from our own garden. As a side benefit, gardening is good exercise and it can become a family and social event.

Gideon Shor, my Jewish tour guide in Israel, told me of a rabbi in Israel who lived to be very old. One reason for his longevity was attributed to his discipline in eating. He ate very little food and in very small amounts. Gideon always reminds me that our bodies do not need as much food as we Americans eat. This is true. We can survive on far less.

The less dependent you can become upon others—including dependence on any type of government assistance—the more content you will be and the more peace you will have. A small garden can help you do that, and it will save on grocery bills as well.

Suggestion 3 - Have additional money on hand for a sudden crisis

Americans are not savers. It seems that when a person has additional income, instead of saving or investing it for increase, they immediately seize an opportunity to spend it. Often they buy things that have little, if any, long term value. With the increase in natural disasters such as hurricanes, earthquakes, and tornadoes, I have taught that each person needs to have some cash set aside in a safe place in the event of an emergency. Months after teaching this in Louisville, Kentucky, a severe winter storm struck the city, downing power lines in some areas for weeks. A woman who heard me teach this had set aside some money. Even though the power was out, she was thankful to have the cash available to make purchases.

People learn this lesson when they are forced to flee cities during natural disasters. When people fled New Orleans during hurricane Katrina, they discovered that when they purchased food and gasoline, the stores needed cash and specifically, small bills. It is good to have ones, fives, and tens instead of larger bills, because the stores might not be able to give change in times like that.

When the electricity goes out, important items cannot be purchased. Gas pumps operate off electricity, although some stations have generators. Even simple purchases are difficult to make when the electric grid or power lines are down. It is not *fear* to make preparations; it is simply *wisdom*.

If economic confusion and high government debt levels persist, one of the great concerns is a possible "run on the banks," similar to the one that occurred during the great depression. Thousands of people went to their banks and demanded their money in cash. Since local banks kept only a certain amount of cash on hand, the sudden withdrawals caused a problem for banks. Many people lost their entire savings. Some older Americans who grew up during the great depression still tend to hide their money elsewhere, as they fear another bank run.

Today there are FDIC protections placed upon deposits, up to a certain amount. But even with precautions that have been put in place since the great depression, banks could not handle many depositors demanding all of their cash at once. In the event of such a crisis, people will be glad they have some cash set aside. Whether it is a run on banks, a national emergency, or a natural disaster, there could be times when it will be difficult or impossible to gain access to cash.

Some people save by putting aside the family's extra change. I recall a survey that was conducted some time ago that indicated the average American family has $38.00 in change around their house! I once decided to collect all the change that we had in our house for a month, and I was surprised at the total. This gave me an idea. At a Partner's Conference I suggested that the partners participate in a "change challenge." They could use change only, and would have several months to collect it and send it to the ministry to assist in a special project. I would give away one of my old preaching Bibles to the person who collected the most change.

I was stunned at the amounts raised, especially by children. One young fellow raised the astonishing amount of two thousand dollars! Two young people whose parents are partners of the ministry raised a combined total of fifteen hundred dollars! The winner raised nearly four thousand dollars. This simple challenge demonstrated to all participants the "power in the change." Nickels, dimes, and quarters might seem like small change, but they add up to dollars, which eventually add up to hundreds or even thousands. To have additional income, sometimes all it takes is discipline, creativity, and determination.

Suggestion 4 - Have additional long term food in storage

There is one religious group in the United States that traces their roots back to the early 1800s. Based upon dreams from their elders, many which occurred before and after the American Civil War, the families have been taught to set aside at least one year's worth of food, in the belief that the day will come when there will be massive food shortages. This group owns some of the largest dried food companies in America. While I do not say this to authenticate their dreams, the idea of having a supply of food is practical and wise in many aspects.

A nationwide drought, major flooding during farming seasons, or other natural disasters could wipe out the food that is grown in California and America's Midwestern and southern states. This would cause food shortages as well as increased food prices. I have heard ministers and other Christians mock the idea of having additional long term food supplies on hand, but these same ministers scoff at or admittedly know little or nothing about the many prophecies in the Bible concerning the time of the end.

As I have shared numerous times with our own staff, if a crisis arose and the news media showed one major city in America where the people were storming a grocery store and the shelves were empty, this would spark a panic and entire cities would be impacted within hours. Just the threat of a snowstorm empties grocery stores of milk and bread.

In large cities, such as New York, many of the people eat out so often that they have only a small supply of food in their apartments. Every day, large trucks transport food to restock restaurants and grocery stores throughout the city. If people woke up one day and found grocery shelves nearly empty and restaurants with limited food, there would be widespread panic in the community among those who are unprepared.

There are places online that sell dried food that is guaranteed to last years if stored properly. Canned goods purchased in grocery stores can last months, or even two to three years. Pay attention to expiration dates, and rotate the food before the shelf life runs out.

People who have survived major storms and earthquakes will tell you how important it is to have water, food, and basic supplies to carry you through the crisis. Pay attention to the area where you live and the possible dangers that could arise there.

This is not being faithless or fearful; it is being prudent. The Scripture reads, *"A prudent man foresees evil and hides himself, but the simple pass on and are punished"* (Prov. 22:3). In Hebrew, the word prudent means to be subtle and cunning in your thinking. You are to think in advance and be wise enough to discern the possibilities and prepare for them. We are told to *"go to the ant, consider her ways and be wise"* (Prov. 6:6). Solomon then comments that the ant will provide its food in the summer and gather its food in the harvest (Prov. 6:6-8). Like the ant, it is prudent to gather food so you will have it when you need it.

Suggestion 5 - Invest in safe investments – watch the scams

This is a very important message for the body of Christ. I am a fourth generation minister and have been around long enough that both time and experience have taught me some things. I have seen that the body of Christ is susceptible to quick money schemes that can consume enormous amounts of their time and turn them away from church attendance and prayer, or end in an embarrassing scam. On several occasions individuals have approached me with an investment idea that guaranteed a quick return of income for the ministry. In each case I have refused to participate.

In two of the cases, the investment proved to be a scam in which Christians lost hundreds of thousands of dollars. For this reason, many years ago we initiated a ministry accountability policy in which one of the statements is that we do not make investments with ministry money. We do ensure the money is placed in the banks to gain interest and be protected; but as far as investing in a get rich quick scheme for the Kingdom of God, we never accept those offers.

The body of Christ is often a prime target for scammers as the tricksters understand two things: the words of Christians are often trusted by other Christians, and there is power in a testimony. One man showed me that he invested $5,000 and got a check back months later for $10,000. But if this investment opportunity was that great, the Wall Street brokers should be dropping truckloads of cash in it. Claims were that this investment, however, was not for Wall Street; it was just for Christians, because the "wealth of the wicked is laid up for the righteous!" No, in fact, this investment was benefiting the scammers who were laying up money in off-shore bank accounts as Christians lost their money through this scheme.

Another scam that has been tried for years is those e-mails from somebody in Africa stating that you have been chosen to receive millions of dollars from a dead Christian whom you have never met. All you must do is send them money and your bank account information, and millions of dollars will be deposited into your bank account.

At this time, there is an "investment" that will allegedly result in a return of billions of dollars for investors, many of whom are Christians, thus making them multi-millionaires overnight. While I certainly hope it is true, there are too many unanswered questions. For several years, the investment has been "coming due any day now." So far, nobody has gotten a return on their investment. Will this be another scam where the only person who becomes wealthy is the one taking money from the investors?

It is always important for Christians, who are very trusting of people and therefore considered easy targets, to do their research and not throw money at something that sounds too good to be true. History proves that if it sounds too good to be true, it probably is.

Suggestion 6 – Form a community watch group

We live in a small neighborhood where no soliciting is permitted and where the neighbors recognize their neighbors and know if strangers are scoping out the place. One evening my neighbor spotted a strange vehicle in the neighborhood. He became suspicious as the driver slowed down in front of each house. My neighbor blocked the street with his car (not necessarily a wise idea), then confronted the men and asked them questions. They appeared nervous and could not answer his questions. He told them, "We watch this neighborhood carefully, and you have two minutes to get out of here because I am calling the police." They immediately left. We all know that people will do anything for money—especially in an economic crisis, or when they need money for drugs. They will break into homes and steal items that can be sold and converted to cash. The elderly and many other innocent people cannot defend themselves from these criminals. This is why I suggest that you become acquainted with all of your neighbors and set in place a community watch. Exchange phone numbers and know the numbers of the police and emergency agencies in your area.

I don't discuss the security measures we have in our office, but if somebody comes in the front door and attempts to physically harm one of the employees, they had better be prepared to face the consequences. We do not take threats lightly. At times we have found it necessary to report certain individuals to high agencies and they were investigated for their threats and actions. In the world's climate with its culture of violence and crime, there is nothing wrong or anti-Biblical with having some form of defense for you or your family. I remind people that in the New Testament era, traveling was done on foot, by animal, or on ships. Traveling could become dangerous, as Paul said he was at times in danger of robbers and dangers in the city (2 Cor. 11:26). When Christ was headed toward the garden before His death, He told His disciples,

"But now, he who has a money bag, let him take it, and likewise a knapsack; and he who has no sword, let him sell his garment and buy one"
(Luke 22:36-37).

The disciples had lacked nothing when they traveled with Christ. However, He was going to leave them, and they needed to make provisions and have a form of protection—a sword.

Individuals have numerous options for protecting themselves and their families. I will not make suggestions concerning what you should do, as each individual situation varies. A person must know the laws of their state concerning such things as small firearms or even pepper spray, and they should be trained by a professional on the proper use of such agents.

Above all, never underestimate the power of prayer! Ask God for the assistance of protective angels over yourself and your family members, and pray a hedge of protection over your family daily. Remember:

"The angel of the LORD encamps all around those who fear Him, and delivers them."
- Psalm 34:7

Suggestion 7 – Learn to hear and follow the voice of the Holy Spirit

It cannot be stressed enough how important it is for a believer to fine tune their spiritual ears to hear the nudges and the inner, still small voice of the Holy Spirit. Christ spoke of the Holy Spirit as the Comforter. The Greek word for comforter is *parakletos*, which indicates one who comes alongside you to help you. Christ said the Spirit will lead you into all truth and show you things to come. He said the Holy Spirit will have a voice and will not speak of himself, but will speak only what He hears the Father say (John 16:13). This truth is evident, as the Holy Spirit is the agent to disclose and enact the will of the heavenly Father on the earth, through God's people!

Many times in our family, prayer kept a tragedy from occurring. My dad could always pray and sense when danger was ahead. He knew when he must listen to the Holy Spirit and change plans or directions. He also knew when it was time to stay on his knees and go into deeper intercession. Because he listened to the Lord and obeyed, there were many times when we escaped an accident or even death. I recall late one night, years ago, when we were traveling and came close to being hit head on by a tractor trailer. But the trucker saw something pick up our car and set it off the side of the road. The entire family walked out of the automobile unharmed, and I believe Dad's intercession before the trip helped save our lives that night.

Sometimes a person will experience an accident or some unexpected negative event and will comment, "I knew I should not have done that. I felt something telling me not to." Secular people often refer to that as intuition or a sixth sense. But a Spirit-filled believer is aware of the fact that God knows the future, and He is speaking a warning through the Holy Spirit. God will help you discern any dangerous steps you might be taking. Learning to hear is the first step, and learning to obey is the next step in following God's will.

Suggestion 8 – Stay in Faith and Not Fear

In the last days, you will have to choose between either crisis or covenant. It is impossible to build your faith level by watching the news every day and worrying about what might occur. There are many talking heads out there, and the news can be seen on several television stations, twenty-four hours a day and seven days a week. To maintain network ratings, they must report conflict, confusion, and bad news to keep viewers glued to their television like a magnet. Everybody wants to know how these events are going to affect them personally.

You must choose between living in the crisis or living by the covenant. When God established His covenant with Israel, He gave a redemptive plan through the blood of a lamb. He gave an economic plan in which the Egyptians provided the Hebrews with gold and silver that were used to construct the wilderness tabernacle. Then He included a healing covenant when He announced that He was the Lord who would heal them, and none of the diseases of Egypt would come upon them (Exod. 15:26). Their provision was available through their obedience to God's revealed covenant.

Believers today must renew and review in their minds the inspired words of the New Covenant, and stand on the many promises provided through the redemptive covenant. Christ promised to never leave us nor forsake us (Heb.13:5), and He said that He would be with us always, even to the end of the age (Matt. 28:20). Paul taught that when we are obedient, God will supply all of our needs according to His riches in glory by Christ Jesus (Phil. 4:19). In order to bring us strength, wisdom, and comfort, we have been blessed with the Holy Spirit who is the "other Comforter" (John 14:16, 26). We are not left without hope, without comfort, without faith, and without a future. This we must never forget.

Finally, in the book of Revelation it speaks about those who refused to take the mark, or worship the beast or his image. We read, *"And they overcame him by the blood of the Lamb, and by the word of their testimony; and they loved not their lives unto the death"* (Rev. 12:11). Notice these martyrs have no fear of dying. Once a believer loses the fear of death, there is absolutely nothing the enemy can hang onto in their lives. Mankind's greatest fear is the fear of dying; and once man loses that fear, the adversary can no longer torment or frighten them.

> *"Inasmuch then as the children have partaken of flesh and blood, He Himself likewise shared in the same, that through death He might destroy him who had the power of death, that is, the devil, and release those who through fear of death were all their lifetime subject to bondage."*
> –Heb. 2:14-15 (NKJV)

A true, redeemed believer cannot be intimidated by the threat of dying and going to heaven. Whether through death or through the catching away, we will enter the heavenly kingdom. Christ has taken the sting of death, and now all believers can sing, "Death where is your sting, grave where is your victory?" (1 Cor. 15:55). Those who refuse the mark, name, and number of the beast, and reject the Antichrist and the lying signs and wonders, will be forced to give up their lives. But they will be permitted to rule and reign with Christ for a thousand years. The future is frightening for the lost, but it is truly exciting for the believer!

CONCLUSION

At this point, the world still does not know exactly what this mark, name, and number of the beast will be. However, we are the first generation since John's vision of the apocalypse that now has the technology and global capability to use numbers and marks to identify a person's every movement—from birth to death, and in between. Through the development of modern technology, individuals are already having chips implanted under their skin to carry their unique information, identity, and even physical location.

The shaking up of the kings and rulers in the Islamic nations is a shifting that will reorganize these prophetic lands under the unification of one man called the Antichrist. As other Islamic nations, especially those surrounding Israel, become more anti-Semitic and call for the destruction of the Jewish State, it will be an indicator to the Believer of an increase in the spirit of lawlessness and the soon appearing of the man of sin (2 Thess. 2:1-9).

Believers should also brace themselves for a time when those of us who believe Jesus is the only way to heaven will be verbally assaulted as being "intolerant, right-wing fundamentalists," and there will be a new emphasis on the importance of unity among all religions. This is the purpose of the false prophet—to unite the major Middle Eastern and all other world religions together, particularly Islam and apostate Christianity.

One of the most common questions is, "Will the church be on earth when this occurs?" The judgment seat of Christ occurs in heaven for the believer in Revelation 11:18, and the beast system is fully emerging when the Antichrist and false prophet invade Jerusalem after killing the two witnesses (Rev. 11:1-10; 13:1-18). Thus we see the heavenly judgment set before the latter part of the tribulation.

Others believe that the gathering together follows the messages to the seven churches in chapter two and three, by the imagery in Revelation 4:1, when John heard a voice like a trumpet saying some up hither and immediately he was in the throne room in heaven. This view is called the pre-tribulation catching away, or rapture.

While I lean toward the pre-tribulation position, I feel that every believer should follow the same pattern of those mentioned in Revelation 12:11:

"They overcame Satan by the blood of the lamb and by the word of their testimony, and they loved not their lives even unto death."

We often preach on overcoming Satan by Christ's blood and by our testimony, but the ultimate key to overcoming is to love not your life, even unto death.

The greatest fear that binds people is the fear of death and the question of where they will spend eternity. Once you know that you are in relationship with Christ and you will be with Him forever, the fear of death can be broken. We can always debate, and we often do debate, the question of whether the church is gathered before, in the middle of, or at the end of the tribulation. However, if we have made up our mind to serve Christ and we have no fear of death, then the fear of the future has no hold over us. Knowing that the best is yet to come is all we need to break the fear of death and eternity!

notes

Chapter 1
Apocalyptic Predictions: The Impossible is Now Possible

1. Augustine, City of God, book 16; 18 chapter 22

2. http://www.eyewitnesstohistory.com/christians.htm

3. http://en.wikipedia.org/wiki/Atomic_bombings_of_Hiroshima_and_Nagasaki

4. http://www.suite101.com/content/roman-tattoos-and-tattoo-removal-a221158

5. www.ancientworlds.net/aw/Post/55599

6. www.xtimeline.com/evt/view.aspx?id=53924

7. www.ancientworlds.net/aw/Post/55599

8. http://www.cnbc.com/id/39886462/Chinese_Computer_Trumps_US_One_as_World_s_Fastest

Chapter 2
The World Must go Global

1. Boak, A. E. R., *Manpower Shortage and the Fall of Rome*, page 39

2. Ibid, page 40

3. Ibid, page 44

4. Ibid, page 48

5. www.wikipedia.org/wiki/Ida_May_Fuller?

6. http://www.nydailynews.com/money/2011/05/14/2011-05-14_new_report_warns_social_security_medicare_could_run_out_of_money_even_earlier_th.html

7. http://www.marketoracle.co.uk/Article25969.html

8. www.asharq-e.com/news.asp?section=3&id=13528

9. The Koran, Surah 4:3

Chapter 3
The Trigger That Will Initiate the Antichrist System

1. http://www.bibletools.org/index.cfm/fuseaction/Bible.show/sVerseID/30800/eVerseID/30800

2. http://www.greenlivingtips.com/articles/223/1/Bees-and-your-food.html

3. Cleveland Daily Banner, May 6, 2011 "Levee blast means lost year for Missouri farmers"

4. http://www.bloomberg.com/news/2011-05-04/rising-corn-prices-threaten-meat-profits-seaboard-says-1-.html

5. Josephus Antiquities; War of the Jews, Book V, chap. III

6. http://www.foreignpolicy.com/articles/2011/04/25/the_new_geopolitics_of_food

7. Josephus Antiquities; War of the Jews, Book V, chapter X

8. Ibid

Chapter 5
The Health Care Tracking Device

1. http://www.youtube.com/watch?v=hgcZUIc3oks

2. http://www.youtube.com/watch?v=n5tczn0mke8

3. http://www.theregister.co.uk/2002/06/10/first_people_injected_with_id/

4. http://www.youtube.com/watch?v=SsqsLm6yMgw&feature=related

5. http://www.youtube.com/watch?v=SZia4FkPR_U

6. http://www.globaltrackinggroup.com/healthcare-facilities-gps.cfm

7. www.antichips.com/press-releases/chipped-pets.html

8. www.antichips.com/cancer/index.html

9. www.weizmann.ac.il/

Chapter 6
God's Judgment on the Seal of Satan

1. http://www.nytimes.com/2009/05/11/world/europe/11golem.html

2. http://www.youtube.com/watch?v=Xguu48_bShk&feature=related

3. http://www.youtube.com/watch?v=thOxW19vsTg

4. http://www.youtube.com/watch?v=qf5esT95Glw

Chapter 7
The Mark and the Symbols – An Islamic View

1. http://www.ancient-hebrew.org/28_chart.html

2. Ibid.

3. http://www.freebsd.nfo.sk/hinduism/symbols.htm

4. Ibid.

5. http://wwrn.org/articles/8653/?&place=russia-cis

6. http://news.bbc.co.uk/2/hi/middle_east/3572325.stm

7. http://www.66619.org/thequran.htm

Chapter 8
Red Dragon Rising – The Coming Mr. Xi

1. Adam Clark Commentary on Revelation 12

2. www.eia.doe.gov/energyexplained/index.cfm?page=oil_home#tab2

3. http://www.economist.com/node/17309197, "China's Next Leader: Xi Who Must be Obeyed"

Chapter 9
Eight Suggestions for Preparing for the Last Days

1. Eusebius, History of the Church, 3:5:3

2. W.E. Vines Expository Dictionary of New Testament Words, page 236